What It Fucking Is

Cindy Sevell
www.itiswhatitfuckingis.com

I'd like to recognize and thank all those who gave a fuck and all those who continue to give a fuck...

My beautiful children, Joshua and Julia, the lights of my life, my reasons for living....

You inspired me to fight the fight. You are my reasons for everything I do. You are the two most precious things in this world to me. Your love and support, no matter how difficult things have been, and they have been, have carried me through my darkest moments. I love you both with everything I am, from deep within my soul. Thank you both for being the two best parts of my life. I fucking love you with all my heart.

My Bestie....

Deb, what can I say. You are the sister I never had. You are my bestie. You have stuck by me for over 30 years, through good times, through bad. Your love is unconditional and I am so grateful to have you in my life. I fucking love you.

My Breastie....

Melissa, you are proof that there's always good to find, no matter how awful things may seem. Breast cancer brought us together and for that I will forever be grateful. I fucking love you, my pink sister.

Kristen Jensen....

My friend...my photographer...Kristen, you came into my life at one of my darkest moments. You brought me light and hope through that beautiful heart of yours. Thank you for sharing my journey with me and encouraging me to begin the next phase of my life. I'll always be grateful. I fucking love you, my friend.

My Twin Soul....

I must thank you for encouraging me to write this book. For whatever reasons, which will remain between us, I was inspired to sit down and write. I wrote and I wrote. I finally succeeded in writing the book I have been wanting to write for years. Thank you for loving me, encouraging me, believing in me and supporting my efforts. I fucking fucking fucking love you and I'm in fucking fucking fucking love with you. Twin Soul love is rare and I feel so fucking blessed to have found it and you.

Random Friends, Family and Strangers….

Thank you to all those who stepped up with offers of love and support. From meals, to hugs, to rides to the doctors offices, to help with my kids, I will never forget all the fucking love and support I was given.

Those Who Didn't Give A Fuck….

I do want to thank all those who didn't give a fuck. You taught me to stand tall, be strong and pull up my big girl panties. I learned I can do anything I fucking want to. I supported myself, I fought cancer myself, I discovered your true colors. These were hard lessons to learn during the most difficult times of my life, but I'm a stronger woman because of it all. So, thank you for not giving a fuck.

My Readers and Supporters….

Thank you for picking up my book, for reading it whether you like it or not. Thank you for dealing with all the fucks I put out there, for understanding that cancer fucking sucks and there is no other way to say it. Now, go read and enjoy the fucking shit out of this book!!

Huge fucking thank you, Susanna Schavoir, for the beautiful cover design. You ROCK.

This book is dedicated to Shila, my hero, my fellow canine cancer survivor, a member of my beautiful family, who continues to inspire me every fucking day. She's been battling osteosarcoma, had a shoulder and leg amputated, went through chemotherapy and a fucking awful clinical trial but her tail still wags, she gets so much love and gives even more in return. She is beautiful, inside and out, and reminds me every day that, "It Is What It Fucking Is".

How do I REALLY feel?!!!!!! Read my poem.....

FUCK you, you FUCKING leach...
You make me sick, you make me weak...
You drain my life, my spirit, my strength...
You make me cry, my pain knows great depth.

Tears forever lingering behind my eyes...
Burning and ready to slip...
I outwardly smile but hurt inside...
You ruined my life you piece of SHIT!

I changed, a few say...
It's all your FUCKING fault...
You tried to kill me...
Without a damn thought.

I resisted and put up a fight...
You came out of nowhere and cornered me...
How dare you barge into my life?!!!
Why not just let me be???!!!

You invaded one breast...
But I gave up two...
Not giving you any chances...
So FUCK off and FUCK YOU!!!

Think that was easy?
Losing both my breasts?
You rocked my world...
But that's all you'll get!

I have my life, I have my hair...
I have my health and those I hold dear...
Those who walked, judged or hated...
Were truly destined to disappear.

You are an ugly part of my life...
You bring me such sorrow and strife...
You knocked me down, left me helpless and defeated...
You forced me to gather the strength I needed.

I'm back on my feet...
My life in MY hands...
Out of your ugly grip...
I'm making my stand.

You opened my eyes, unclogged my ears...
You shook me to my very core...
My bubble was burst, true colors displayed...
Manipulation, control, abuse NO MORE.

NO ONE will hold hostage my spirit...
NO ONE will change who I am...
Despite your unwelcome ugliness...
You're part of God's big plan.

Despite the darkness you forced upon me...
A lot of light shines through...
Those who stood beside me showed me...
Love, support, kindness and truth.

You LOST. I won, the battle of LIFE...
I gained a new perspective...
I choose happiness, laughter, unconditional love...
Honesty, truth and all things respective.

Love wrapped it's arms around me...
Lifted me, carried me...
Protected me from all that was meaningless and false...
The truths have finally set me free.

So FUCK YOU CANCER, you fucked with me...
I'm back on my feet, albeit battered and bruised...
You left your marks, emotionally and physically...
Watch your fucking back...you're fucking screwed!

Chapter Fucking 1
A Leaky Tit

A leaky tit catapulted my life into the pits of depression, poverty and loss.

Leaky tit – classy, right? How else do you describe a tit that's leaking? Oozing? Disgusting? Yes. Scary? You bet your fucking ass it's scary!

If you can't handle foul language, please put this book down now. It's only going to get worse from here. The word "fuck" took on a new meaning once I was diagnosed with breast cancer. Fucking breast cancer fucked up my life for close to four fucking years. That's a lot of "fucks" in one sentence, isn't it?!

Let's go back in time a bit. I'm going to tell you a fucking story that will blow your fucking minds. Being diagnosed with breast cancer, or any cancer for that matter, seems so commonplace these days, but it was something new to me. It totally rocked my little fucking world.

The day was May 15th, 2015. That's a lot of 5's. 5/15/15. A Friday I will never forget. I spent close to three hours in Dr. Beth Sieling's office, my breast surgeon, trying to understand my diagnosis and my options. In fucking tears. By the way, what surgeon spends close to three hours with you? Mine. Beth was wonderful. Bottom line, the only option I had was to live. I chose to do whatever I had to in order to survive and be here for my children.

May 21st, 2015 – It was my forty-fifth birthday. I was miserable. So incredibly sad. Lost. My mother made a delicious breakfast for Josh, Julia and I – warm fresh crepes with dulce de leche, a variety of fresh fruit, whip cream, coffee and juice. Early afternoon, my mother and I went to Starbucks for a cup of coffee. I wasn't feeling it but we went regardless. As we were walking in, I ran into some clients of mine. My mother walked in to order for herself while I was chatting with them. A couple of local police officers happened to be standing outside and overheard our conversation. I happened to know them from town given I owned a local business. They told me they overheard my conversation, wished me a happy birthday and told me they were sorry to hear about my cancer. I walked into the store and sat down with my Mom and my clients. Around twenty minutes later, one of the police officers went back into Starbucks, bought a gift card unbeknownst to me and gave it to me as he was walking back out. I'll never forget that act of kindness. This was from a family man, with tons of kids which equated to tons of bills. He stopped in front of my Mom, my clients and myself, and said, "I hope this can bring a smile and brighten your day a bit. I'm sorry for all you're going through." He then gave me the gift card. I was in complete shock that this kind man took it upon himself to perform such a gracious act. It did in fact put a smile on my face. It's amazing what one act of kindness can do.

Later that evening, my mom, Josh, Julia and I went out for a delicious dinner to celebrate some more. The sadness permeated my entire being no matter what. The tears were still there, randomly slipping out. Sadness engulfed me but it was nice to have my kids and my Mom with me.

May 27th, 2015, I lost both of my beautiful but unhealthy breasts. Double fucking mastectomy. I loved those breasts as they were part of who I was. They were part of my femininity. Within six hours, they were gone. I woke up with small hard expanders in their place and no nipples. I woke up a new woman in many ways, forced to deal with life's god awful curve balls.

June 2nd, 2015, after losing my breasts, I lost my family. How does that happen, you wonder? I have no fucking clue! People work in mysterious ways and life's hardest moments can sometimes bring out the fucking worst in those you never expected. Little did I know how difficult my life would become, like it wasn't difficult enough to deal with a cancer diagnosis.

Back to June 2nd, 2015. I woke up, got dressed and went downstairs in search of my mother. Well, Mom was nowhere in sight. I called out, "Mom? Mom. Where are you? I'm ready to go to the surgeon." No response. I finally figured out that she wasn't at my house as she was supposed to be. She forgot about my post surgical follow up appointment so I decided to drive myself. Now, mind you, my license was in her purse. I was in no condition to be driving but all I could think was, "I need to get checked by the doctor." So, I left. I got in my car and drove myself to the surgeon which was 10 minutes away. I didn't take the pain meds that morning so I didn't feel groggy although I was very weak. When they cut off your boobs they cut through all your chest muscles. No one told me I wouldn't be able to lift my arms! Well, I hit a branch that was hanging low with my passenger side view mirror and broke it off. That sucked. But, I successfully got to my plastic surgeon, who ended up being the biggest bitch and butcher I have ever had the misfortune of meeting.

June 2nd, little did I know, my mother took off. I was back home, in bed, exhausted and resting. My mother arrived home at some point and all of a sudden, I hear a suitcase being rolled out of her room. I ask, "Mom, where are you going?" She replied, as any loving mother would, "I'm leaving. Your cancer is stressing out your sister and I'm worried about her. I'm going to take care of her."

Wait a hot fucking minute here. My cancer is stressing out my estranged sister? Are you fucking serious? Sure, I chose to have cancer. Wait, I also wanted to lose my breasts. I couldn't fucking wait to go through a six hour major surgery and experience the incredible amounts of physical and emotional pain I endured. And you know why I did all this? Because I wanted to stress out the absolute worst sister I could ever dream of having. It was planned! Revenge baby!!!

Ok, back to reality here. I was laying in bed, in pain physically, suffering emotionally as well, just wanting the love and support of my mother yet she elected to choose one daughter over the other. How do you choose one child over another? How do you abandon your own kid during a time like this? I couldn't wrap my head around this.

I spent two fucking devastating weeks pacing my bedroom in tears, trying to understand something I couldn't understand, trying to make sense of something so unimaginable and so unexpected. Did she have her reasons? Who the fuck knows. Was there any reason to abandon your child during the toughest time of her life? NO. NO FUCKING WAY.

Now, let's not forget my Dad. Dad never bothered to leave Florida to be with his daughter. Isn't that normal? No. I would think any parent would drop everything for their child. At least that's how I work. I figured my parents would at least be there to support my kids and I. After all, I was their daughter! Little did I know how selfish they truly were. Little did I know how little I truly meant to them. Little did I know I'd be traveling this journey pretty much alone. I had one constant in my life and that was my daughter. My daughter stuck by my side through everything.

Life without boobs and family carried on despite my physical limitations and my emotional lows. After getting a couple of professional opinions, I learned they removed all the cancer and there was no need for meds that would force me into early menopause, no need for chemo and no need for radiation. Truly, a reason to celebrate in the midst of such terrible times.

The summer was upon us at this time. Summer of 2015 was well under way. I sent a text to my father, who I hadn't seen since before my diagnosis and surgery, wishing him a Happy Father's Day, despite the fact that he wasn't speaking with me and he was acting like the worst Dad ever. His response to me was that he was moving their things out of my house which I so graciously stored for them the past three plus years given they moved out of state. I had given them the guest room, keys and alarm codes so they could come and go as they pleased. Anytime they wanted to visit CT, they had a free place to stay. Fuck me!

Upon learning they were searching online for men with muscles and a truck to move things out of my house, I respectfully requested they hire movers that were licensed and insured. Simple fucking request. I was a single mother with two young children, living alone. Instead, they called my attorney and the police – state AND local. In fact, not only did they call the police but they went to the police station when they were in town to ask to have me arrested. Arrested for what? Storing their shit in my house for 3 plus years for FREE? Allowing them to stay in my house for FREE? The police all finally realized how absurd the situation was and agreed I should only have a licensed and insured mover in my home. I arranged for that licensed and insured mover myself given the task seemed too daunting for them (took all of 10 minutes on the internet to arrange!) and their things were moved out three days after the last police threat of being arrested.

Not one, not two, but three fucking cop cars were outside my house that day of the move thanks to "Dad". State AND local police cars loitered outside my house. Now, that's love. My best friend and sister, Deb, happened to be at my house that Sunday. She grew up with my family and was in complete shock. She could not believe what was happening. A large intimidating police officer knocked at my door that Sunday and asked to come in with a serious "don't fuck with me face". He wanted to see everything that was being moved, per my "father's" request. I was in tears, shaking visibly, ready to collapse, but explained to this particular police officer all that happened. This large emotionless man was in complete shock after hearing that my own parents would treat me like this. It was beyond stressful and embarrassing.

If you can't control someone, destroy them. That was their philosophy. Well, guess the fuck what? It didn't work.

The summer went by. I had serious complications with my expanders. December 7, 2015, I had the boob exchange. I received my first set of implants. Why the first set? Because, if you recall, I mentioned the bitch of a butcher of a plastic surgeon. I was sick that very night with a high fever and a swollen right breast. I ended up in the hospital with a serious infection within the next day. I was on IV antibiotics and another $14,000 worth of antibiotics that didn't work. They were so strong, they made me pass out while driving, shopping, etc. But that infection never went away. And, that butcher bitch didn't give a shit. She left those implants inside me despite all of the problems.

During a follow up visit with the bitchy butcher plastic surgeon, I asked her about evening out the breasts given the swollen one appeared to be twice the size of the other. She, in her normally rude and inconsiderate manner, replied, "We'll see". What? We'll see?? Wrong fucking answer! Especially when I was told in my initial consultations that there would be some fat transfer if needed to even things out. I replied, "Wait, what do you mean, we'll see?" She replied, "We'll see." I was in shock. She then so kindly added, "Face it, yours was a difficult surgery. You had large droopy boobs." Yes, that bitch called my breasts, "droopy boobs". I can call them boobs. She can't. They weren't droopy but pendulous. And they were beautiful. How dare this bitch insult me because she couldn't face the fact that she fucked me up?!

Bitchy Butcher walked out of the exam room and the tears started to fall down my cheeks. I stood there, feeling so vulnerable, alone, topless, in the room. She disrespected and insulted me in so many inappropriate ways. I left in tears, made my next follow up appointment and drove home. As soon as I got home, I decided I'd never go back there. I called to cancel my appointment and arranged to pick up a copy of my medical file.

Time for a 2nd opinion. New York City was first. I brought my daughter with me because I was honestly too afraid to go by myself. Having my 12 year old daughter with me forced me to be brave. We took the train in, somehow found the office, went shopping and had lunch. That day meant more to me than my beautiful daughter will ever know.

The New York City triple board certified plastic surgeon wouldn't accept my insurance so I kept searching. I found another woman in Fairfield that offered to do the surgery for me for free. Yes, for FUCKING free. Breast reconstruction was all she did. She felt awful for me given I was so botched. Insurance wouldn't approve of it given she was not a participating provider under my plan.

The search continued and I found the incredible plastic surgeon I now have. He gave me hope that I would one day look and feel more complete. I had six more fucking surgeries over the course of close to three years...eight surgeries in total because of the bitchy butcher.

Now you ask, what happened to the family? They came and went. I tried but neither could actually own up and apologize. I neglected to mention my brother. He was part of those who abandoned me. I wasn't the only one they hurt. My kids were hurting and felt abandoned. They were torn.

Single mother of two diagnosed at age 44 with DCIS/IDC Stage 1A. Single mother turns 45 six days later. Single mother ends lousy relationship to focus on what's really important in life. Single mother loses both her breasts six days after her 45th birthday. Six days later, single mother loses her family. Until writing this, I never realized that there may be some symbolism in the series of 6's. The devil was hard at work! Three 6's can't be coincidental. Why the fuck would the devil have an issue with me?! I'd like to take a moment to describe the sort of person I am. Yes, I'm swearing a lot in this book but that's not how I typically speak in person. I'm swearing for the obvious reasons – cancer just fucked up my life as I knew it. It fucked up my body. It fucked up my family. And all of that fucked with my heart and my head.

Chapter Fucking 2
Life Continues

Four years of hell ended, thankfully. But, let's go back in time a bit. I owned a tanning salon/boutique in the next town over which was a dream come true for me. It wasn't a big moneymaker but it was a passion of mine. A huge accomplishment. Surgery after surgery after fucking surgery didn't allow me to work for long periods of time. Eventually, I had to close my business and fell behind with payments. Financially, I was suffering. Breast cancer organizations so graciously helped me a little after I showed them I was falling behind. What an embarrassing and vulnerable position to be in, to literally beg for help. I was on my own and realized I had to do what I had to do. I couldn't lose the house. I couldn't end up on the streets. I had 2 kids in the forefront of my mind and lots of determination despite all the odds and hurdles I had to overcome.

Mystique Boutique and Tanning was closed permanently in December of 2016. I got a job selling cars. Well, four months of that hell was more than enough. During that time, I took quite a fall on a soaking wet floor inside the dealership. That fall resulted in the need for a double knee replacement. When I finally felt my life was coming together, it fell apart on me all over again. We'll get into more of that later.

What do you do when someone potentially gives you a death sentence? You do everything you ever wanted to fucking do! Life is too fucking short not to. So, I decided I wanted to ride a motorcycle. Me. Girly me. On a bike. Now that's quite a sight! I bought a Harley no less. If you're going to ride, you better ride a Harley! My first bike (hell yea, I had the Harley itch!) was a beautifully kept 2008 Sportster 1200 with just over 4k miles. It sat in my garage for a bit until I took the motorcycle safety class. I took the class three weeks after yet another breast surgery and fucking failed. I left that weekend long class exhausted and crying yet proud that I never fell off or dropped the bike. I had never ridden any sort of motorized two wheel vehicle on my own and I didn't even ride a bicycle!

For a few days, I walked past my bike in the garage, feeling intimidated. One day, I said, "Fuck it! I've got to ride!" I took the bike out and went up and down my street. Every single day. At least 20 to 30 times a day, pissing off the snooty neighbors but getting more and more comfortable with the bike. I decided I better get my permit so I could ride the streets legally. I got my permit. I practiced the heck out of that thing. I renewed my permit two months later and practiced some more. Returning to the class was vital given I had to pass their course before getting my license. Surprising the instructors, I returned and even better, I passed. Barely, but I did it! I rode everywhere, every chance I had. I rode until my knees wouldn't let me ride anymore.

I should add a little interesting side note here. In order to pass, the worst grade you could get was a "15". A "15" meant you messed up 15 times during the exam. The best score you could get was a "0" which meant you did a perfect job. You'd think with a max of 15 errors, they give you a lot of wiggle room but I more than doubled that number and scored a whopping and seriously failing score of "31" during my first go around. Heck, when I do it, I do it right! The second attempt, I scored within passing range but as I mentioned, barely within. My second score was a "13". I was so relieved – it was a close one, but I did it!

Given I loved riding, I chose to get a part time job at a local Harley dealership. One day a week sufficed. Immersing myself into the Harley culture was the idea, meeting new people with similar interests, getting great discounts on items I needed and a new healthy social outlet. I made some dear lifelong friends I have to this day while working there. It also brought me deeper into the biker community in ways I never would have expected.

Sweet suburban college educated girl turned biker bitch. Now that's fucking hysterical! I still looked like the girly girl I am. I rode with a dress over my jeans and boots. Rockin' my own style, I entered a world I knew nothing about. Fun was an understatement. Soon after working at the Harley dealership, a man in his late forties with blonde hair and blue eyes walked in. He sweet talked me into going out with him. He didn't really look the "biker type" but he was wearing his "colors". He was part of a local biker club but didn't really have that typical biker look. We ended up dating for a short time and that's how it all began. During that time, I was introduced to others which led me in a completely new direction. Within a few months, I ended it with him, which was the best thing to do and ended up joining a ladies club. Now, I was truly the girly girl of the group. Did I really belong? Hell, no. There were only five members when I joined and I was the fifth. A couple more members joined after me and during that time I realized it wasn't the life for me. They wanted to change me. I didn't want to change. I wanted to be accepted for who and what I am. I loved and still love who I am. I was expected to change who I was to conform to their requirements. No fucking way.

This Jewish girl went to lady biker "church" one day in March and turned in her "colors". Yes, can you imagine me, wearing colors? For those of you who don't know what that means, it's that leather vest you see bikers wear with patches on the front and back, labeling you with the name of your club. Felt fucking incredible to turn those colors in. Nothing and no one controls me. Nothing and no one will change who I am. My search for a sense of family, given mine walked out on me, led me to this group of women I had nothing in common with except for one fabulous woman who also left. A sisterhood sounded promising. Love, support and acceptance of each other but none of that existed. It was full of control and jealousies. I learned on my own that I loved to ride but I didn't like being a part of the club life. My kids were relieved I gave it up. My family, as well. I neglected to mention that there were attempts on both parts, mine and theirs, to reconcile. Unsuccessfully, at that time.

Chapter Fucking 3
And Continues...

The Sportster 1200 was sold and I bought a 1992 Heritage that is absolutely beautiful. It wasn't working when I bought it but with time and a little bit of money, I got it up and running. Truly, a classic in every way. Colors, class and age. A huge bike for me which I did dump twice but heck, still a huge accomplishment for me!

I got a new job in a field I never thought I'd be in for no other reason other than I never realized it existed. Two days after another major breast surgery, while I was recuperating in bed, I received a call for a job interview. They wanted to meet me that day. I couldn't. I wasn't in any shape to go on a job interview but I thought, this could be my chance for a new career in a new field. I psyched myself up to go interview the next day. I was all bandaged up, weak and tried to dress appropriately considering all this. I explained to those interviewing me that I had just had major surgery but wanted to meet with them and was very seriously interested in the position. I drove to a hotel in Milford, CT, to meet with them. My daughter came along with me for support and waited in the car while I went inside.

Needless to say, I got the job. Sales and marketing in senior living. I loved what I did but I can't say I felt appreciated in the place I worked. I was able to combine my sales skills along with my compassion, making a difference in people's lives. It taught me a lot about life, getting old and about death. Empty promises were made there, people came and left all the time, quit or got fired, truly a revolving door, personalities clashed and bullies were allowed to be bullies. I decided to secretly interview elsewhere. With the experience I now had, I knew I'd find something else in a better community and would be paid what I was worth.

Life went on, I took some falls from my knees that were giving out on me due to that nasty fall at the car dealership. I tried out for a calendar. Me. LMAO! No naked pictures, no worries! It was a classy 50's pin up calendar supporting a cause near and dear to my heart. Through the sale of the calendar, we raised money to help stomp out domestic violence. I should input a little piece of info here…..I was abused by my ex-husband for 14 plus years. So, this calendar was a wonderful way for me to help support others AND give me a wonderful sense of accomplishment. Who would have thought I, Cindy, would be a Calendar Girl?! Miss June 2019.

Accomplishments. I'm all about them. Life is too short. After the cancer diagnosis, I knew I had to tackle everything on my bucket list. Tomorrow is unknown and I told myself that when it's my time to go, I NEVER want to regret the things I DIDN'T do – if there are any regrets, it would be for the things I DID do. That meant I was LIVING. ALIVE. LOVING LIFE.

Karate – somehow I managed to get my Apprentice Red Belt in Tang Soo Do prior to my breast cancer diagnosis.

Now, that's hysterical! I was yelled at all the time for apologizing to my counterparts as I sparred with them. I couldn't stand hurting anyone. Now, breaking a cement block with my bare foot was pretty wild as was breaking tons of flaming wood. But, karate was not for me. Especially considering the woman, my "friend" who was sleeping with my husband at the time, loved to beat me up.

Flying – I flew Cessna 172's for a while, just before my cancer diagnosis. I had to stop because I just didn't have the upper body strength to fly after my double mastectomy nor did I have the extra money. Flying is downright expensive. I was getting pretty good at it after a while and was aiming to get my private pilot's license. Of course, I did well with the instructor sitting next to me. Lol!

Motorcycle Riding (mentioned earlier but worthy of mentioning again!) – something I always wanted to do but was never "allowed" to during my marriage. I finally fucking did it! This bad ass chick knows how to live it up. Notice the key word "live". Life is meant to be lived. I realized I was given a second chance and I wasn't going to waste a single minute of it. This was a huge accomplishment of mine and so exhilarating.

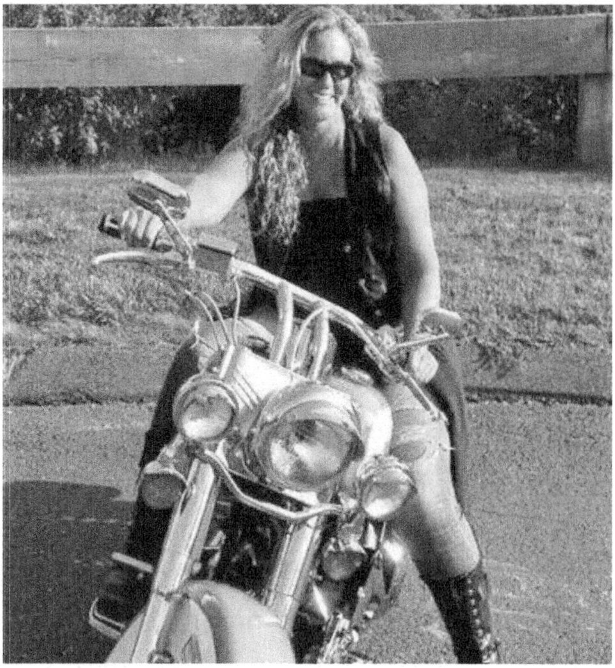

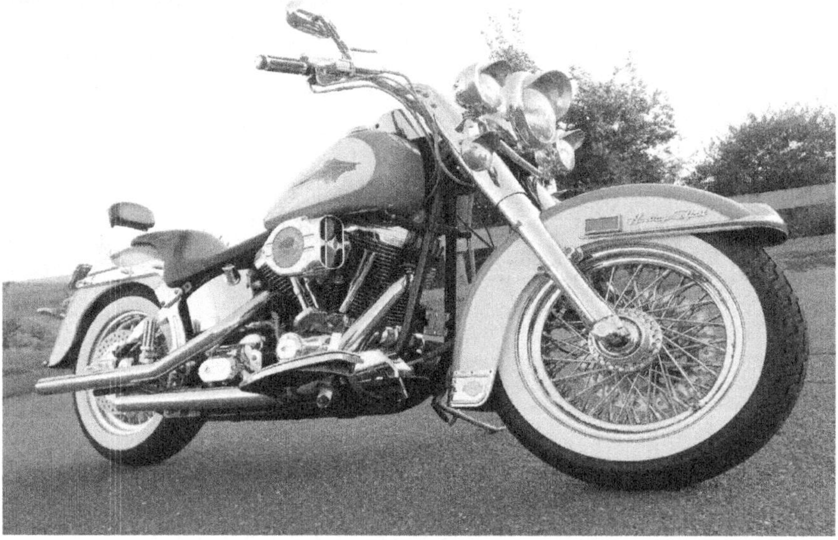

Chapter Fucking 4
The Day They Cut Off My Beautiful Breasts

How does one prepare mentally for an amputation?

I have no fucking clue. I do know that I couldn't stop crying.

I woke that morning with swollen eyes, of course, anxious to rid the cancer from my body but nervous, nauseous and deathly afraid.

I went to the hospital early that morning and was brought into a little room to get undressed and prepped for surgery. Dr. Beth Sieling came in and sat with me, many times, trying to console me. She knew how scared I was. I was a fucking wreck. This was so fucking surreal. All of a sudden, it was happening. I was going to lose my fucking breasts. Beth didn't rush me. Beth genuinely cared.

Dr. Beth Sieling followed me closely the entire year after she formally met the leaky tit. Listen, leaky tits don't just happen every fucking day. She ordered a shit ton of tests yet everything came back "inconclusive". Dr. Beth Sieling would never settle for "inconclusive" so she persisted until she was able to find something to test. Thank the fuck lord she did.

Dr. Beth Sieling knew how much I loved my breasts. The very first time I met her, the very first time she examined me, I told her. In fact, every single time I saw her, I told her. Beth was impressed with my decision to have a double mastectomy given she knew how much I loved those puppies. They were beautiful. Despite it being my ultimate decision, and the most radical, she told me it was the best decision. I trusted her sound advice and am so grateful that I did.

Beth always made me feel so comfortable. She was and remains a real, down to earth person. I always left her office with all of my questions answered and fully understanding our next steps. That's fucking empowering, ladies! She never rushed me and she always explained everything. When I was finally diagnosed with breast cancer, she said confidently, "We're going to get that fucking shit out of your body!" Yes, people, Beth actually loves the word "fuck", too!!!

Cancer won't fuck with this breast surgeon. Look how beautifully fierce she is!

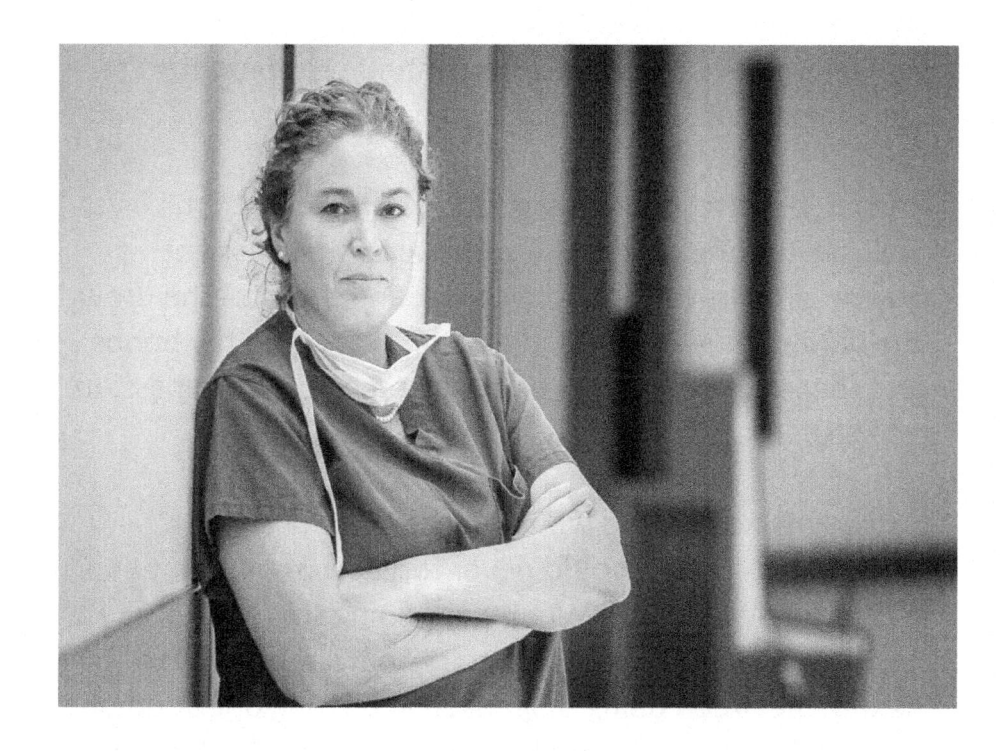

Pictured is the amazing Dr. Beth A. Sieling, MD, FACS
Surgical Breast Specialist
Division Chief Breast Surgery, Saint Mary's Hospital

Beth was the compassionate one, the surgeon who gave a shit. She was the one who sat with me for three fucking hours on a Friday night and explained all of my options, in great detail, after she had to share my awful news. Beth was the one who opened up her office on a fucking Saturday to see me, in between her kids' sports games, because she was worried about me and wanted to see me right away. Beth became a friend through it all. Dr. Beth Sieling is loved and respected by so many because she treats each and every one of her patients as if they are family, because she is real, because she cares. I was so blessed to have found her and continue to count my blessings to this very day. She helped save my life.

The bitchy butcher of a plastic surgeon met with me as well. No fucking compassion. She took a permanent marker and drew all over my chest and breasts. She drew the outline they were to take when cutting off my boobs and she left. No words of encouragement, no compassion, no eye contact, no fucking nothing.

I asked my Mom, who was with me, to take a before surgery picture so I would never forget that moment. It all felt so fucking surreal! What was I doing there? How did this happen so fast? I was grateful I only needed to wait 12 days between being diagnosed and being operated on, but the day was here and I was freaking out. My beautiful beautiful breasts. I was going to lose them within minutes. I was going to wake up a completely different woman.

I was so nervous that I kept having to pee. I would lay back down in the bed only to feel that urge. I'd get up, make my way to the bathroom with the IV machine wheeling alongside me – I was all hooked up and ready to go. I went three or four times within a matter of 15 or 20 minutes, finally realizing it was nerves. During my last visit to the bathroom, I looked at my breasts and I said my goodbyes. I lifted each one up and gave them a parting kiss. Does that sound fucking weird? I don't fucking care. It felt right at the moment. Those breasts were mine. They were a part of me since fucking puberty and I fucking loved them.

I was finally fucking ready. I went back to the bed and called in the troops, who were waiting on my readiness. I say "troops" because there was a lot of fucking medical staff involved in this six hour major surgery!

The beautiful thing about anesthesia is that one minute you're up and the next minute, you're completely out. My six hour long major fucking painful surgery went by, it seemed, within seconds. At least, to me. Not for my loved ones who were waiting for me. The next thing I knew, I woke up in a hospital bed, all wrapped up in a beautiful pink Velcro halter top, drugged up and delirious. No pain whatsoever thanks to very strong meds. I woke up happy, smiling, unaware of what just happened. I actually looked quite beautiful given my hair never got messed up, I was tan and I was sporting that beautiful pink top. I recall looking down and seeing BOOBS! What the fuck?! Did I really have the surgery? I must have! They look smaller! But, I have BOOBS. Wait, what the fuck happened? Am I dreaming all this? Am I so drugged up that I am seeing something that's really not fucking there?

I was so happy. Flower fucking child happy. I loved everyone. Of course, the drugs enhanced all this. I was crying and miserable going into this surgery but I woke with a smile on my face and love to share. I HAD BOOBS!!!

Ok, no, I didn't have any fucking boobs. I had what they call "expanders". The first half of my surgery, the amputation by the amazeballs Dr. Beth Sieling, the removal of my beautiful breasts, took three long fucking hours. The second part of my surgery, the first step of reconstruction by the fucking bitchy butcher plastic surgeon, was the placement of my expanders. These expanders are hard mounds that get filled with saline and are placed under my chest muscles. They are meant to "expand" the space behind my chest muscles in order to make room for the implants.

Let's discuss expanders. Expanders fucking hurt. They are like hard fucking rocks inside your chest. I used to hurt my daughter every time I hugged her. Those fuckers are hard! Every few weeks I went back to the bitchy butcher of a PS (Plastic Surgeon or Piece of Shit) and she injected saline via a needle, through my skin and into the port. She inflated those suckers little by little until she felt there was enough room for the obnoxious implants she intended to use. That's another chapter in itself!

I went home after a couple of days. The pain meds wore off right at the time I arrived home. Excruciatingly fuckingly painful can't even describe the pain I felt. I cried in pain as I made my way up to my bedroom, blindly walking to the place I knew I needed to be. My bed. I took the pain meds and waited in agony until they started to kick in. This fucking sucked. Reality sunk in when the pain meds wore off. I had breast cancer. I fucking lost my breasts.

I couldn't lift my arms. I had no strength. I was weak, tired, in so much fucking pain. I couldn't even pretend to be social. How the fuck was I going to get through this?

Chapter Fucking 5
Expanders in Fucking Detail

I previously mentioned what the expanders are and what their purpose is. Let me tell you what happened with mine.

My expanders were inserted behind my chest muscles just after the double mastectomy. The beginning of my reconstruction took three hours that day, following the three hours it took to remove my breasts. Expanders are hard. They hurt inside. They are supposed to be fucking TEMPORARY. Well, the fucking douchebag of a plastic surgeon decided she wanted me to wait for my implants...and wait...and wait...and wait. She claimed the implants she wanted to use weren't available yet. She wanted to use these "gummy bear" high projectile fucking shitty ass largest implants on the market. The problem was that they were too large for my body, they were textured and they were not what I wanted. Whose boobs were they anyway?! Seriously! I begged her to use the round implants and to get the surgery done sooner, as it SHOULD have been done.

The expanders were heavy and painful. They started moving around, rubbing against my chest wall, stretching my skin, rotating and flipping backwards. That fucking hurt – it took my breath away and had me doubled over in pain! I looked completely deformed. It was beyond ridiculous. This wasn't fucking normal and that bitchy butcher of a plastic whore could give two fucking flying shits.

I begged that bitch to get my implants. Finally, in December of 2015, I received my first fucked up set of gummy projectile missiles/implants. Everything that could possibly go wrong that day, did. The morning before, my parents attended a counseling session with Kelly, my counselor, and I. I learned then that my mother wanted me to have peace if I died – she wanted me to reach out to my fucking nasty ass "sister". She kept pushing and pushing, as did my brother and my father. I hadn't talked to my "sister" in over five years. What made them think I gave two shits about her at that time? I didn't! I was at fucking peace with my decision from five years past. My parents felt some guilt, I'm sure, and asked to be at the hospital the next day. I agreed. It was beyond awkward.

I let them come into the prep room with me. I was prepped and given my IV. They gave me vancomycin intravenously, an antibiotic prior to surgery. I knew immediately something was wrong. My arm started to burn. It started to itch. It started to throb in serious pain. My heart started to race. My head started to itch. I was frantically scratching my scalp but nothing was helping. I was turning red everywhere. My Mother thought I was losing my mind, because, of course, she thought I was crazy, when in fact, I was having an awful fucking allergic reaction to the vancomycin! RED MAN'S SYNDROME. I called in the nurse and told her I'm having some serious reactions. They immediately realized what it was, tried to reverse the reactions and eventually, the pain and swelling and itchiness and racing heart subsided. Talk about fucking scary!

I go into surgery. I come out with implants. That very night, my right breast began to turn red and swell. I had a high fever. I was very worried so I called the bitchy butcher's office. She wasn't worried and claimed it was probably due to the anesthesia.

I documented my fever. My right breast swelled even more. I called again the next day and by the evening, per my suggestion, I was admitted to the hospital. I was given IV antibiotics and met with an infectious disease physician. I had cellulitis and was given some very serious antibiotics. $14,000 worth! And guess the fuck what?! It didn't fucking work! That bacteria entered my breast at the hospital during my botched surgery and stuck to the grooves on the textured implant. I should have had that implant removed ASAP.

Bitchy butcher wasn't worried. My new amazing plastic surgeon was! He started by removing my implants as the bitchy butcher should have done in the first place.

I proceeded to have six more surgeries with this amazing plastic surgeon. He was knowledgeable, talented and kind. Guess what type of implants I ended up getting, per his recommendation? ROUND. ROUND FUCKERS! JUST LIKE I ASKED THE BITCHY BUTCHER FOR!!!

Chapter FUCKING 6
The Word FUCK

FUCK.

That's my all time favorite word! FUCK FUCK FUCK.

Fuck adds the appropriate amount of emphasis to anything you say. This is so FUCKING good. This FUCKING sucks. FUCK you. Get the FUCK outta here!

My favorite saying which got me through my fucking breast cancer is........and it's tattooed on my foot...yes...it really is.....

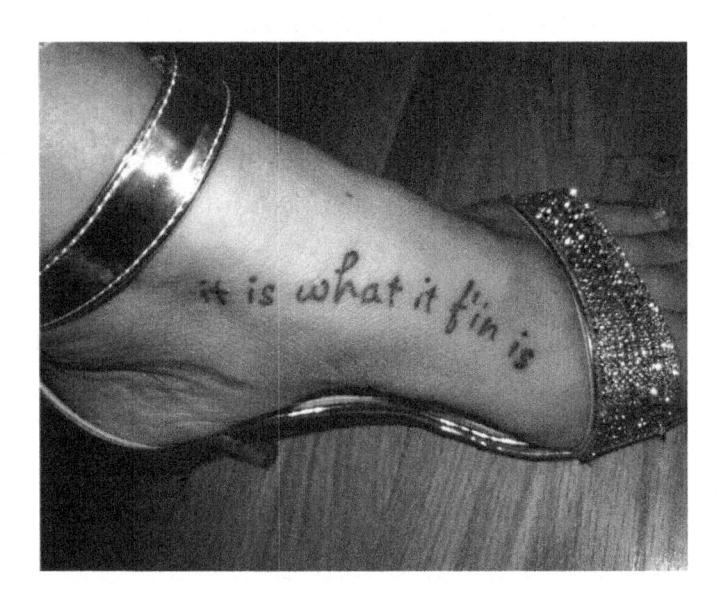

"It is what it FUCKING is....."

Sometimes, when you just can't understand why things happen the way they do and it's hard to fathom, you can say to yourself, "It is what it fucking is!" I'll share my favorite quote with you if it can help put your fucking pain to rest. It fucking helped me! Those two weeks wandering around my bedroom immediately after my double mastectomy and being abandoned by my family, I finally said, "It is what it FUCKING is". I decided I couldn't waste any more time trying to understand something that made no sense whatsoever.

As my botched surgeries by my first FUCKER of a plastic surgeon became very apparent and as my fucked up reality sunk in, the need for another plastic surgeon along with many more surgeries, the fact that I couldn't fucking work and I was fucking alone, my fucking bills were piling the fuck up, my fucking business was on the brink of fucking disaster, my boobs or lack of took on all fucking sizes and shapes, my depression fucking plummeted, I just kept uttering those beautiful words, "It is what it FUCKING is".

You can do it too! Try it!! Say it – "It is what it FUCKING is." Now, yell it out, "IT IS WHAT IT FUCKING IS!" Tattoo it on your foot like I did. Write it on your mirror. Post it notes everywhere. Whatever the FUCK it takes to help you deal and heal. FUCK everyone. You need to make yourself a priority. You need to learn how to heal and keep moving the fuck forward!

One day, while working for a senior living community, I received a call from a woman in a nursing home. She wanted information so instead of mailing it, I decided to go visit her with cookies, flowers and all of the info. We sat and chatted for a bit. She was dying, unbeknownst to both of us. She had no family. She had very few friends. So, I asked her if there was anything she needed. She told me she wished she had thought to bring her lipstick. She missed her lipstick. I left that day and decided to go shopping and buy her a lipstick in a shade that would light up her face. I found the perfect fucking color. The lipstick case was a sexy red with the word "Sexy" on it. I thought, perfect! The very next day, I went to visit her again at the nursing home. I got out of my car, took the Sexy lipstick out of the bag and as I was ready to walk into the building, I took a quick look at the lipstick in my hand. Well, there were a few other words on the lipstick that I must have missed given I was so focused on getting the right fucking color.

Sit down for this one. I'm bringing a beautiful shade of pink lipstick into a nursing home for an 85 year old woman. It's already a little riske with the word "sexy" on it. Imagine this one…..

"SEXY MOTHER PUCKER"! Holy shit! What the fuck do I do?! Do I return this lipstick and go search for another one? Fuck no! I spent 45 fucking minutes trying to find the right shade for her skin tone. I thought, who doesn't want to be called "SEXY MOTHER PUCKER" anyway! I sucked it up, walked in, sat down in her room and after a little small talk, told her I had a little gift for her. I told her I bought her a lipstick, which I hope she liked. The problem being, when I bought it, I didn't realize what the brand was. I was more concerned about the color. I then told her, "YOU are SEXY AS A MOTHER PUCKER!" This 85 year old woman stared at me for a second, a complete stranger (ME) holding out a brand new lipstick, and started cracking the fuck up! Thank GOD!

Soon after, I found out she passed away. I went to visit her a couple more times beforehand and each and every time, she had on her SEXY MOTHER PUCKER lipstick. That made me feel fucking wonderful, knowing that something as simple as a lipstick could make a woman feel so much better.

Isn't that what we should do in life? Reach the FUCK out to others? Be FUCKING human?

So, as you can see, Mother Fucker/Mother Pucker – same fucking thing. Isn't that FUCK word amazing? Even in disguise on a fucking lipstick for an 85 year old dying woman!

My gorgeous daughter designed the most fuckingly fabulous shirt for my birthday one year during the height of my cancer journey. Pink. Of fucking course! The breast cancer color. How the fuck she did this, I'll never know. Most places wouldn't print up my favorite fucking saying. But she found someone to do it! She had my t-shirt printed with, "It is what it fucking is." She included all the words that brought me strength. She included her birthday, my son's birthday and my birthday. She thought of all the truly important things to include on that t-shirt. I laughed when I opened that gift. I cried, too. I will treasure that gift forever. My teenage daughter understood how this saying got me through life's difficult moments.

IT IS WHAT IT FUCKING IS.

FUCKETY FUCK FUCK.

Fuck. Such a liberating word!!!!!

FUCK YOU CANCER!!!

You can go fuck yourself.

Fuck yourself in your fucking ass!!!

Chapter Fucking 7
Julia, My Amazing Daughter

Julia.

Julia stood by me throughout absolutely EVERYTHING. She was 12 when I was diagnosed with breast cancer. Sadly, I wasn't the one to notify her of my breast cancer diagnosis, my own fucking daughter. It was robbed of me like the fucking thief my sister is. My "sister" and I have never gotten along. She overstepped her boundaries all the fucking time. This is how it happened.

It was a Friday, May 15th, 2015. I went to see my amazeballs breast surgeon, Dr. Beth Sieling, 10 days after that god awful biopsy. I knew it was bad news. It was a very long 10 day wait as you can imagine. It was around 4:45 pm or so when we sat down in the room she consulted in. We sat down together at a round table and of course, despite thinking the worst, I NEVER fucking expected to hear it!!! I heard those dreaded words, "You have breast cancer." What the fuck! I'm going to die! How the FUCK will I be able to keep the house for the kids? How can I afford to support my kids if I can't work?! I can't die! All of these initial thoughts crashed through my head upon hearing those words. I started to cry and I couldn't stop. I couldn't believe it. I had fucking cancer! What the FUCK! I never bought anything pink that supported breast cancer because of a stupid fucking fear that I would "catch" it! I couldn't even LOOK at anything pink that supported breast cancer causes. I was so afraid of "catching" it. Superthefuckstitious! Seriously, what the fuck?! How ironic – I'm the one to get it.

My amazeballs breast surgeon, Dr. Beth Sieling, who followed me for a year since my leaky tit discovery, sat with me for close to THREE FUCKING HOURS! Who the fuck does that?! She stayed on a Friday night, counseling me, explaining my options to me, comforting me. I was all alone. I'm fucking crying as I'm typing this. I'll never ever forget that feeling. I left armed with information, enough that I didn't even feel the need to "google" it. She presented all my options, which was best, which was ok, which she suggested despite it ultimately being my own decision. I left there like a deer in headlights. Tears couldn't fucking stop. I had to go back to my tanning salon to spray tan a couple of clients. I text my mother on the way, saying, "DCIS with IDC. I'll talk to you later." I couldn't talk. I was in tears. I was an emotional wreck. I'm lucky I could even see to spray tan these women that waited hours for me to return. I had no clue I'd be at the doctor's for that long. They understood I had just received the most awful news given I contacted my employee to notify her of my extreme lateness.

My son knew something was wrong. He text me over and over and over asking me what the doctor said. I told him I'd talk to him when I got home. I couldn't lie and tell him everything was ok. I'm no fucking liar. I couldn't tell him I had fucking breast cancer. Not by fucking text! So, he knew. My mother then did what most families would do – she notified my siblings. That's dandy and all but my sister hadn't been in my life for the previous five years. She was a bitch, still is for that matter. My brother brought his kids to my house, was there for support and ordered pizzas. Because pizzas fucking help when you're depressed. LOL! It was such a kind gesture.

I pulled into the driveway. My brother and my handsome son, Joshua, didn't even let me get out of the car. My brother knew because my mom told him, of course. My son didn't. I told him then, in a very calm manner. I explained all of my options. He was very concerned about the Tamoxifen. I asked how he knew about that medicine. He said his teacher had breast cancer and had to take it. Josh was so supportive and told me he knew I'd be ok.

I walked into the house. Julia was playing with her cousins. Those FUCKING tears were fighting to escape my eyes so I went upstairs to my bedroom, closed my fucking door and called my mom. I was bawling my eyes out with her. Just then, Julia opens the door with tears in her eyes, eyes wide open in shock and the phone up to my face. My fucking "sister" sent my beautiful daughter a text telling her that I HAD BREAST CANCER. What the FUCK?!!! Who the fuck was she to take that away from me?! This is MY FUCKING DAUGHTER! This is MY FUCKING ISSUE! This is MY FUCKING FAMILY! I tell my kids MY fucked up news the way I fucking want! My poor daughter. NOT the way she should have found out. I went crazy on the phone with my mother, telling her what happened and telling her to tell my "sister" to butt the fuck out of my life!

I held Julia, consoled her and explained what the doctor said. That little 12 year old girl was so afraid to lose her mom. Julia and I are two of the same, she's my mini me. She went through a bitter divorce to learn her mother, who she has always been so close with, had cancer. She had nightmares. She had those nightmares for years where she would yell out in the middle of the night while fast asleep, "Mommy!!!! Mommy!!!!!!!!!!!" She would dream that I died. It was devastating and broke my heart. To know my kids suffered so much breaks my heart to this day.

Cancer physically and emotionally fucks up not just the person it inhabits, but emotionally fucks up those who truly love that person.

Julia stood by me throughout each and every surgery. She saw my breasts, or lack of, take all different shapes and sizes.

1. Real boobs with nipples.
2. Post double mastectomy boobs with hard expanders and no more nipples.
3. First set of horrible implants by the bitchy butcher and no nipples.
4. No more fucking anything. Flat chested as a baby boy. Disgusting excess skin everywhere. No nipples. Just ugliness. Necessary implant removal by new wonderful plastic surgeon.
5. Second set of implants and no nipples.

6. Four more breast surgeries requiring fat transfers, cuts and lots of stitching and of course no nipples.
7. Tattoos came after all 8 major breast surgeries. Full tattoo coverage. Still no nipples.

Julia saw me topless quite often. She saw me lay flat on my back healing, she'd see my breasts lose and then take shape again. She told me after the tattoos, that I can walk around topless anywhere given it looks like I have a top on! She often consoled me and told me I'm more than my breasts. She suffered alongside me although I didn't always fully realize how much. BUT, she stood by me the ENTIRE FUCKING TIME. She's my girl. She's one of the two loves of my life. She's stronger than she will ever realize. She was and remains my ROCK.

Thank you, Julia, for being the only one in my family to stick by me no matter what. That's love. That's the true definition of family. I like to think I taught you well but you, my love, are one of my heroes and continue to teach me.

Chapter Fucking 8
Josh, My Handsome Son

Josh.

My beautiful little curly headed first born.

Josh was 15 when I was diagnosed. He had a horrible time going through the divorce. It was an ugly bitter divorce. He suffered the most, sadly.

Josh appeared to be rather stoic, strong, he was the man of the house! He must have taken on that role in his mind, that he will take care of things.

But Josh was 15, scarred from that divorce, a teenager and that in itself should say a whole fucking lot. Video games were his thing at the time. Lots and lots of video games.

Josh was so supportive, but scared. Josh, my 15 year old son, helped me wash my hair just days after my double mastectomy given I couldn't lift my own arms to do it. I bent my head over the tub and this boy of mine didn't know what to do. It was a bit comical but we figured it out together. I will NEVER forget how he helped me.

Unfortunately, Josh was extremely vulnerable and easily influenced by my family and his father. After they walked out of my life, it was easy to blame the person with the cancer. Strength in numbers, I suppose. What I didn't fully understand at the time were the fears he had, the tears he cried every night, afraid I might die. The scenarios he played in his mind every night – the "what ifs" he later told me about. My heart broke when he moved out of the house. My kids and I were always so close.

I couldn't understand it.

Those two fucking awful weeks alone in my bedroom, crying non-stop, in physical and emotional pain, I mourned the loss of many things. I lost my breasts. I lost my family. I LOST MY SON! That was the absolute fucking WORST!!!!!

Without getting into too many unnecessary details, it took approximately one long fucking year to get my son back. One night, at our house, we hashed it out. We both cried. We both yelled. We both hugged. We both apologized. And, we both made up. My son told me then, "Mommy, I feel like we are closer now than we have ever been." My apologies were something he NEEDED to hear. He told me that very night. I was so immersed in my own miseries that I didn't quite understand his.

From that moment on, our relationship grew closer and closer. We hit an obstacle but through love and patience, we were able to overcome it.

Josh is the man of the house. He's come to many of my surgeries. He loves me. I love him. With all my heart.

Life hadn't been easy for either of my kids. All I can pray is that this awful journey brought strength to all of us.

My son continues to make me proud. Josh grew up to be a loving 6'2" handsome young man with a full beard, excelling in college, responsible and starting to loosen up a little. His conservative ways are starting to relax a bit, thanks to college, new experiences, living on his own at school and a wonderful girlfriend.

I'm so FUCKING proud of the young man he has grown into.

And, I love him with all my heart.

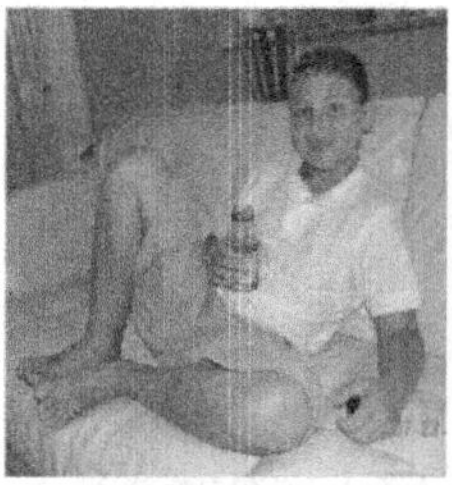
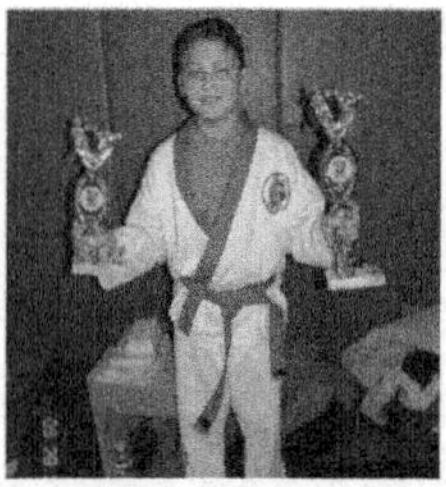
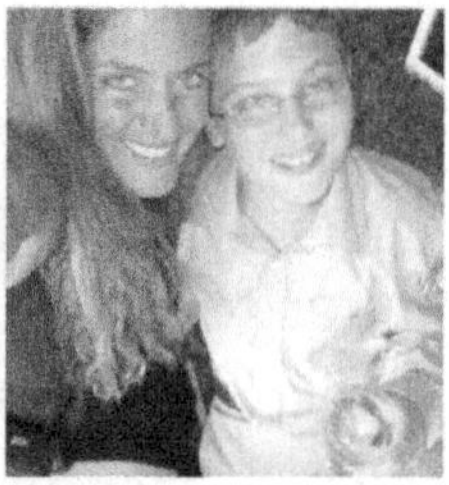
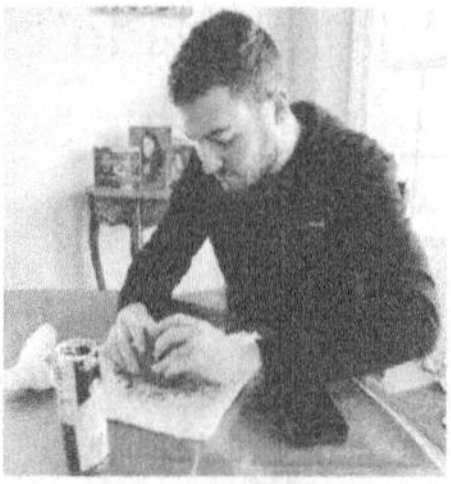
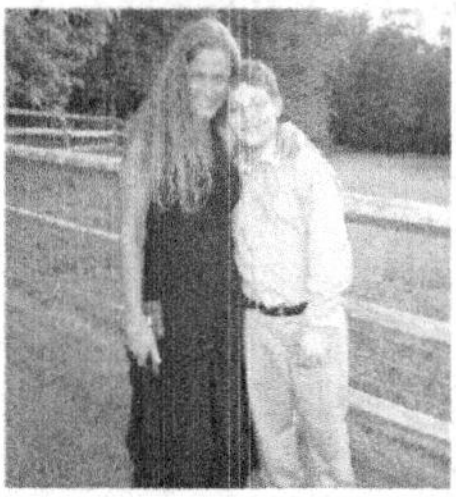
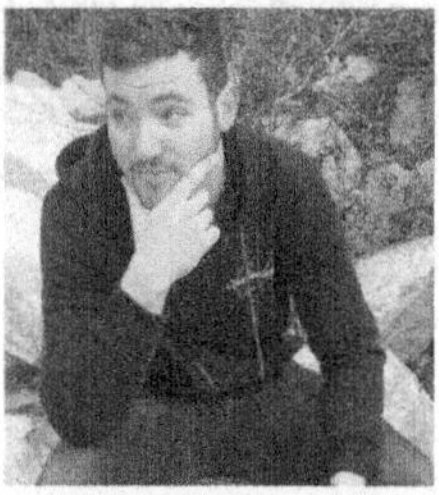
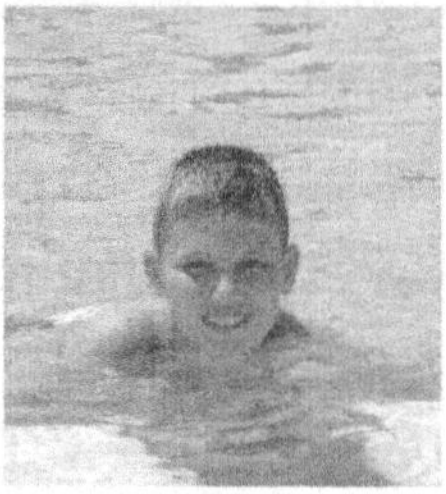
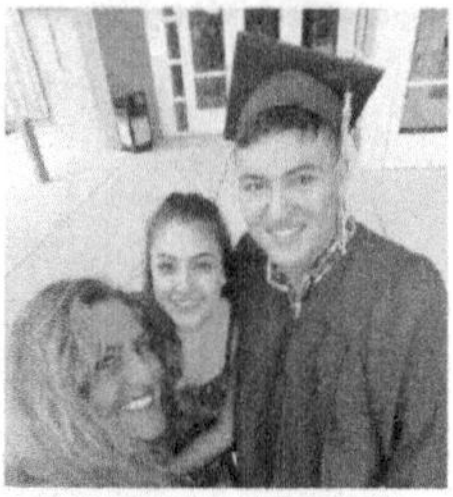
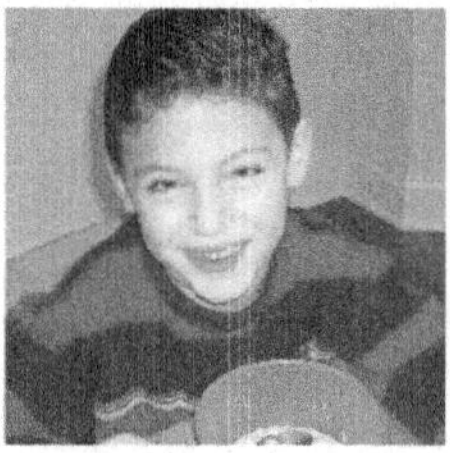
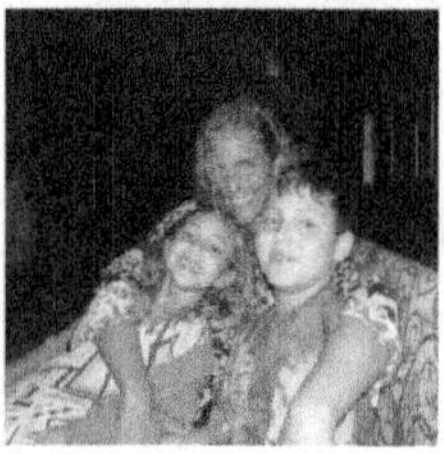
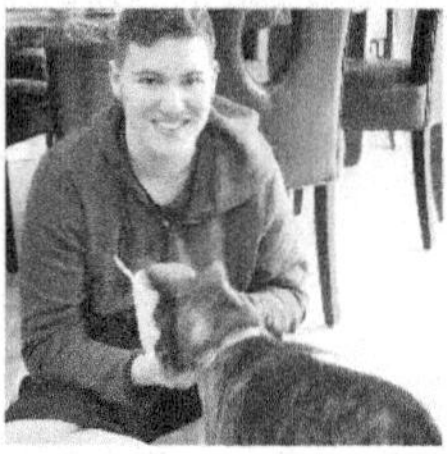
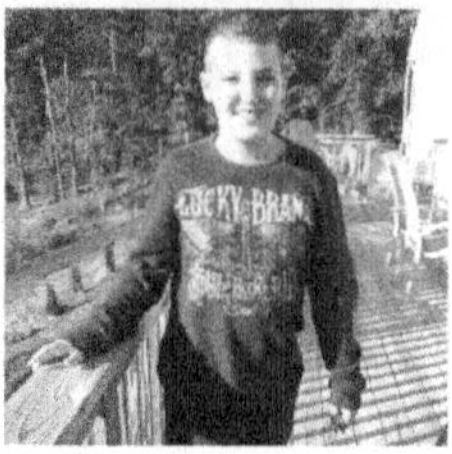
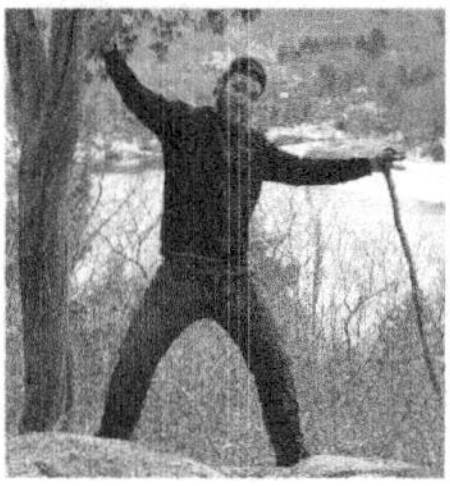
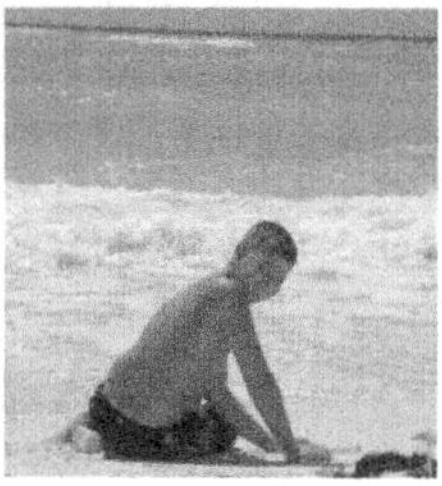
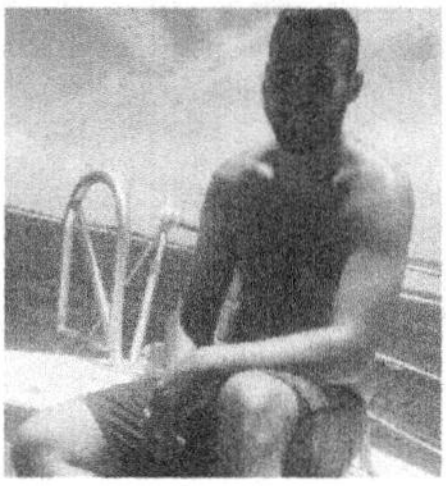
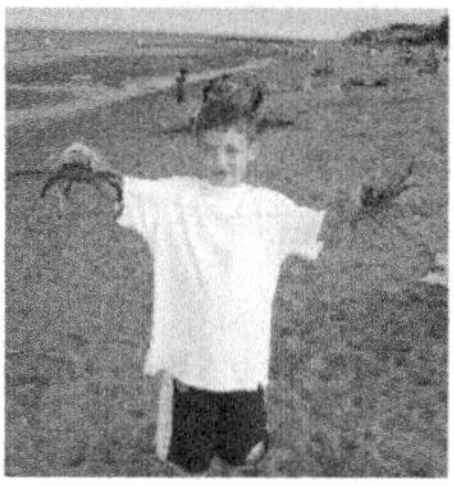

Chapter Fucking 9
Oh My Poor Nipple Rolled Onto The Floor

This is a fucking funny story!

When I was first diagnosed with breast cancer, an old high school friend of mine stopped by my shop to give me a little support. She was recently diagnosed herself and had just had a double mastectomy. She showed me what the expanders looked like, had me feel them (yes, I felt her up!) and gave me as much moral support as possible. She then shared a fucking funny story with me.

This friend of mine was petite, very small breasted and was able to keep her nipples. She had a nipple sparing double mastectomy. After surgery, she was home, recuperating. One day, while in the kitchen with her family, dressed in a loose robe for comfort, she felt something odd and looked down.

Holy fucking shit! Her nipple fell off! Yes, this is a TRUE fucking story, people!! Her nipple fell off, landed on the floor, rolled away from her and the family dog ran after it. She's screaming at the top of her lungs, "MY NIPPLE! MY NIPPLE! STOP THAT DOG – HE'S EATING MY NIPPLE!!"

She frantically ran after the dog, trying to save the rollaway nipple. The entire family ran after the dog to save her rollaway nipple.

The dog fucking ATE it. Yes, the dog ate her nipple.

She was in hysterics. She called her surgeon, left a message explaining her terrible situation, that her nipple fell off and the dog ate it. She was horrified, absolutely beyond devastated.

They were prepared to sift through the dog shit once the dog took a shit to save that nipple. Thankfully, the surgeon eventually called back and informed her that she, in fact, did not lose her nipple. The skin died, similar to a sunburn, and the old skin fell off. Her nipple was still intact and would regenerate the color in time.

Now, this story had me cracking up. There's always humor to be found, even in the most uncomfortable situations. The visual is fucking funny!!

Chapter Fucking 10
Finances FUCKING Sucked

January of 2013, I fulfilled a dream of mine. I opened up a tanning salon and boutique. I had been a Realtor, still am, but felt I wanted to pursue this. Another accomplishment! Sort of. I suppose some accomplishments don't end up as financial successes, in the end. Every successful person makes a mistake or two, right?!

Tanning salons don't really bring in a shitload of money. It's a tough business but a wonderful business. It's a "feel good" business. People always left feeling so good. There's nothing like 12 minutes in a warm tanning bed, feeling that dose of Vitamin D coursing throughout your body, warming up your bones.

I'm going to stop you right the fuck here. NO, I didn't get breast cancer from my tanning. Let's NOT EVEN GO THERE.

My philosophy is this – I never had pockets so I used my left bra/boob as a pocket for my cell phone, for YEARS. Over 20 years. Ironically, or not so ironically, my LEFT BOOB had the breast cancer. I truly believe that my cell phone caused my breast cancer!

Back to my tanning salon. Mystique Boutique and Tanning. My spiritual dream come true. I offered tanning beds of all types and levels, spray tans hand applied by yours fucking truly, gifts of all types and spiritual goods as well. I loved my shop.

The fucking problem was that once I had my fucking double mastectomy, I couldn't fucking work! I couldn't lift my arms so I couldn't spray tan anyone. I couldn't clean the tanning beds. I lost more and more money. Ultimately, I lost my business, owing a shitload of money.

Am I sorry I opened the salon? Sometimes. But, it was a dream I fulfilled. A costly one in the end but of course, I had no intentions of losing it due to an illness I never could have predicted.

So FUCK YOU cancer. You stole my business as well. I was forced to make a decision and the best decision at the time was to close it. December 2016, Mystique Boutique and Tanning closed it's doors forever.

Chapter Fucking 11
Boobless Dating

How does that work out for ya? Dating with no boobs? I'll tell you how it worked out for me!

It didn't for quite a while. I met fucking asshole after fucking asshole. There were some nice ones mixed in but no one I wanted to date more than that initial meeting.

Just prior to being diagnosed, I was "seeing" an asshole named Paul. I have to use his first name, at the very least, because it's a way to call him out on it without getting caught up in legalities. FUCK YOU PAUL. He was a selfish prick. He once told me, "I make a lot of money but I'm not spending it on you." Who the fuck says that?!

He drank a LOT. Wine was his thing. We didn't love each other. It was more fun nights out. Dating. Nothing serious but we weren't dating anyone else. He knew I had horrible news. He offered to pick me up for a drink that Saturday night, May 16th, 2015. He NEVER picked me up. He lived 15 minutes from my house and was lazy and selfish as fuck! So, we went out.

Here is a tidbit of info you don't yet know about me. I don't drink. Never have. One time drunk in college taught me it's an awful thing that makes me feel shitty. Never got drunk again and don't have a tolerance for alcohol.

Remember what the fucking prick said to me? That he makes a lot of money but won't spend it on me? Well, he took me out for a drink. He didn't think to ask if I ate anything that day. I did NOT. I cried all day. I ate NOTHING. So, the FREE chips and salsa came to our table and we BOTH ordered drinks. I thought, what the fuck! Maybe I SHOULD drink and numb these awful feelings I have.

Our drinks came and the FREE chips and salsa were already finished. I was starving. All of a sudden, he started to laugh. He was hysterically laughing. I asked him, "Paul, what's so funny?" No fucking jokes were being told. Nothing fucking funny was said. Well, this was this asshole's response...

Get ready for this one....

"I never fucked a girl with cancer before!!!"

That was the LAST time I ever saw that fucktard! How the fuck dare he?! Karma is a BITCH, Paul. May you get yours!!!

I was actually relieved. I knew he was selfish and I knew I had to focus on what was important at the time. My kids. My health. My life. My finances. I had too much on my plate to worry about some fucked up excuse of an asshole.

I dated here and there. Some very gracious. Others not so much. I recall one loser telling me he would never want to see my breasts as they were because if we were to connect, he would be scarred from seeing them. Are you fucking serious?! Then others begged me to see them. FUCK THAT! I'm no fucking science experiment! Dating was sparse.

I ended up getting into a couple of relationships during the four year cancer journey. The first of the two didn't last very long. He was an asshole of a prick, biker dude. He hid behind his big noisy bike and a cocky undeserving ego. I mentioned him in an earlier chapter, the one I met at the Harley dealership.

I NEVER showed him my breasts. He was as selfish as Paul was, told me he loved me and introduced me to his uptight parents, but it went nowhere. Then I met yet another biker I dated on and off for far too long. This one had nothing to do with biker clubs but he was a hot fucking mess. The one good thing about him was that he respected me for all I went through and accepted my mutilated body as it was. He was still a hot fucking mess who dumped me surgery after surgery, dumped me on my birthday or any holiday, owed me money and spoke worse than I do in this book. Yes, people, that's fucking possible!

Fast forward to today (which may very well change by the time this is published...for good or bad, I have no clue!)

I found my twin soul. How rare is that?! The connection we felt at our very first date is something I will never forget, never had nor can ever duplicate with anyone else. He's tall, he's handsome, he's sexy, he's strong and he loves my breasts because he loves me. He admires my strength. He's multifaceted. He's intelligent, he's street smart, he keeps me safe and he, too, loves the word "fuck". Life with your twin soul isn't always easy! Two people from two completely different walks of life coming together can be a fucking mess BUT despite a few messes, that Twin Soul love is stronger than any issue that can arise. And that Twin Soul love is a love most never find.

So yes, dating without boobs IS an option, ladies!!! Men, we are MORE than our boobs, as my gorgeous daughter always reminded me!

My hope for myself and for everyone else out there is that you have someone to love and support you when things get difficult, no matter what those things may be. I didn't have a whole lot of love and support as I went through my shit. I didn't have a man by my side to love and support me. I once laid in bed after my double mastectomy, after my family left me, and turned onto my left side (which was so hard to do after each and every one of my surgeries), crying, closed my eyes, imagined my man (imaginary of course!) laying next to me, arms wrapped around me, comforting me, silently telling me it's going to be ok, I'm with you, I love you and support you. I didn't have that and I longed for it. I went through so much alone. Sure, I learned how fucking strong I am. But, I didn't WANT to be strong. I didn't WANT to feel so alone. It fucking sucked. No other way to put it.

Tell you the fuck what.....this affected me so much that I felt the need to reach out to other breast cancer survivors.

One day, I had a party at my house for the first of those two selfish assholes I mentioned. It was a surprise 50th bday party (although I'm sure he knew about it and let me spend the thousand bucks I didn't have to spend on it, he cut the grass that one time only because it was for his "surprise party" and bought some Bud because the Sam Adams I bought wasn't really a beer for bikers!) and a woman was coming to the party who I didn't yet know. I found out she was just diagnosed with breast cancer and my heart went out to her. I took a chance! I approached her at the beginning of the party, introduced myself properly and told her that it's really none of my business, but I heard that she was just diagnosed with breast cancer. I had breast cancer and was in the midst of all of my surgeries. She broke down and cried to me. With me. I had a bag full of breast cancer themed gifts to give her, hugs and tears to share. We talked for quite some time. We cried. We bonded. Pink sister love. BREASTIES FOREVER!!

Melissa is my breastie. She has become a lifelong friend that I will always be there for. She ended up having a lumpectomy followed by chemo and radiation. I sat with her in the hospital any chance I had while she got her chemo. I brought flowers or little gifts – one day she said, "Cindy, you don't have to keep bringing me gifts! I just love that you're here." We have both been through so much and continue to be there for each other.

Look for the silver linings, the good that comes from the bad....it's always there to find if you look for it. Melissa, my breastie, is one of my silver linings and I'll love and treasure her forever. She has been there for me as I have been there for her.

Lifelong breasties.

A message from Melissa that truly warmed my heart:

"I lost my hair and my career to this horrible disease. I lost my ability to support myself and I lost the house my kids grew up in, but I've gained so much, too. I have a beautiful granddaughter, a spirit that now knows there's nothing I can't do, I have a deep connection and understanding of all my beautiful sisters who are starting their fight and who have lost their fight. It was at this time that you reached out to me, Cindy. Despite having never met before, we formed an instant bond. Your warm smile and engulfing hug, the handful of mugs and bracelets you gave me and most of all your words of encouragement and experience of having just gone through it resonated with me. Breasties. We have a friendship that's grown into a sisterhood. There is no way I can ever thank you or express what that kind act, that comes so naturally to you, did to change me, my life and my ability to just be quiet. I needed to listen to what God was trying to teach me in this journey. It's because of your inner strength, Cindy. You put yourself out there to a total stranger and taught me that it's ok to reach out to others. The possibility of an undesirable response, the dreaded fuck you, fuck off and what the fuck do you know didn't scare me anymore. You selflessly opened yourself up to me about one of the worst things a woman can go through. You offered your friendship and your advice. Through this, you inspired me to do the very same thing for others that you have done for me. Fear of rejection is one of the most vulnerable feelings a human being can have, but when I saw you toss that aside like it was a fucking throw pillow, I thought to

myself, FUCK IT! If it meant so much to me, and I can help one person the way you've helped me, it's worth a thousand go fuck yourselves! So, my Breastie, you are a fighter, a giver, a true friend and a sister. You are an inspiration that lights up the room when you enter and I will never ever forget what you gave me that day with one simple act that took a shit ton of courage. I am blessed to have you in my life. If just one reader gains the strength to reach out, then I will have tipped the iceberg in my attempt to give another what you have given me. That's all anyone can really do...learn, grow and be a better version of the person they were yesterday. I love you, my dear friend, and am so very proud of you for always being yourself no matter what!!"

Thankfully, Melissa loves the "fuck" word, too!

Chapter Fucking 12
The Fucking Tornado

May 15, 2018, the fucking tornado hit. Yes, a real fucking tornado. Like my life hasn't been a fucking tornado as it was...or my bedroom for that matter! That fucking tornado hit the SAME fucking time on the SAME fucking day on the 3 YEAR ANNIVERSARY of hearing the words, "You have breast cancer." What the fuck?!!!! This tornado hit my hometown, a town where we never see tornadoes. What sort of fucking luck is that?! Close to $70k in damage, 10 days without power, one full year until the house was fixed, it was an absolute catastrophe!

I had my check up with my amazing plastic surgeon that very morning, went to work, received a fucking warning on my phone, heard my officemate ask her kids to bring in the deck furniture so I did the same with my kids. My son was outside with bungee cords securing whatever was too big to bring in. He was short ONE FUCKING BUNGEE CORD. THANK THE FUCK LORD!!! He found one more, turned around to go back onto the deck, saw that everything turned pitch black outside (at 4:45 pm!) and then saw the huge 300 pound grill dancing in mid-air, back and forth, until the tornado crashed it through the deck and flung it mercilessly to the ground a couple of floors down. He said, "Mommy, that was sooooo cooooolllll!!! I'll never forget that!!!!!" Meanwhile, I was shaking at the thought that my son almost had the same outcome as that grill and that deck!

What irony – three years to the day and time I received my cancer diagnosis, my house gets hit by a FUCKING tornado!

Things could always be worse. Thank goodness it was just a tornado!

Chapter Fucking 13
Lucky 13 – Bull Fucking Shit!

I'm fucking skipping this chapter so just fucking turn the page.

Chapter Fucking 14
Oncologists, Chemo, Tamoxifen and Other Shit

Approximately one fucking month after my double mastectomy, I had to go see an oncologist. I had my first appointment with this woman where she told me I didn't need chemo. I already figured as much given only one lymph node turned blue during the double mastectomy. Upon testing it, they found that the cancer didn't spread, thank god. I asked about the Tamoxifen given my cancer was hormone receptive and I was still menstruating. She told me, "If you want to take it, take it." I told her I didn't want to. Guess what her fucking response was? "Then don't take it." I told her she's the professional and I'd love her professional advice. Her "professional advice" was, "You can do whatever you want."

What the serious fuck?! I asked her if we could shelf this for a bit so I can think about it, research it a bit more. She said fine, let's reconvene in one month. One month later, I go back to her office. She comes into my exam room and asks me what I want to do. I still had NO FUCKING CLUE!!! Tamoxifen is scary shit! To help try and prevent one problem, it can cause a whole host of other serious medical conditions.

She said, "You were supposed to come back with a decision." I told her that I still didn't know what to do. I needed her professional advice. She told me to do whatever I wanted. I didn't know what to do so I took the script for the Tamoxifen and left in serious fucking tears. I filled the script and took those awful meds for a few days. I then stopped the meds and called my wonderful amazeballs breast surgeon, Dr. Beth Sieling, to recommend another oncologist for a second opinion. She referred Dr. Michael Cohenuram.

I made an appointment with Dr. Michael Cohenuram, a fucking fabulous oncologist in Danbury, CT. Dr. Mike was thorough and treated me like he would treat his wife. He gave me advice as he would give his wife. Dr. Mike literally told me, "If you were my wife, and I love her, this is what I would suggest." Now, that's GOOD FUCKING ADVICE from someone who took the time to examine me, discuss my medical history, my current situation and discuss the pros and cons of taking the medicine vs not taking the medicine.

Final outcome – Dr. Mike told me, "You're too healthy to take this medicine. You would only cut your chances of breast cancer returning by one percent if you took it yet you would increase your chances of other cancers and blood clots immeasurably if you do take it. If you were my wife, and remember, I love her, I would advise you NOT to take the Tamoxifen and I hope I never see you in here again!!!" Now, THAT is an awesome Oncologist! Dr. Mike took his time, weighed everything out, discussed all potential risks vs benefits with me, examined me unlike the other bitchy lady and made me feel more secure about the decision NOT to take that horrible pill! I left there so happy, feeling so good about going for that second opinion.

People, I have learned something invaluable through my experiences.

Learn from my experiences.

GET A SECOND OPINION IF YOU HAVE ANY DOUBTS!!!

Pictured is Dr. Michael Cohenuram, MD, the most wonderful oncologist and hematologist I have ever had the good fortune of meeting. If you are ever in need of his services, go see him. He truly listens to you, he cares and he excels at what he does. Call it a sixth sense or something, but he's absolutely amazing.

Chapter Fucking 15
Fear The Cancer Will Fucking Return

Fear that the cancer will return is a normal fear.

I had a little skin growth below my throat and immediately had it removed. It wasn't cancer but I was so afraid it might have been. I sat in that general surgeon's chair soooo incredibly excited that he was removing it that day. I begged him to. I begged him not to make me wait. He said he had never had anyone literally fucking EXCITED to get cut open! I wanted that festering shit removed ASAP. I knew I wouldn't have peace until I knew it was out of me, tested and cleared. As he cut me open, relief poured through me, knowing that I was being pro-active with my health and praying that everything turned out ok. Thank god it did!

Blood tests – CA125, the cancer marker….it was elevated and re-tested. Back to normal. White blood cell count and so many other tests – OMFG – could it be back?

Aches and pains – is it the cancer? Did it spread?? Did it metastasize?

Meeting long time survivors always gave me and continues to give me hope. I can do it, too! Hearing potentially scary news is like a sucker punch in your gut. I WILL be a fucking success story and live long enough to share my story with generations to come!

Piece of advice – I can't say, "Don't stress, don't be afraid, don't fear the worst" because if I did, I'd be a hypocrite. I do stress. I am afraid. I do fear the worst. But I will advise you to stay on top of your health. Go to all of your doctor appointments. If anything looks off, address it immediately. You have more chances if you deal with it as soon as possible.

Chapter Fucking 16
Life and How It Fucking Evolves

The journey sucked but the destination is amazing!!!

Fast forward to right this very minute, as I sit here typing, over four years after my breast cancer diagnosis, I can affirmatively tell you that it DOES get better!

My family is back in my life in some form or another. My relationship with my children is even better than it ever was. My professional career took on a new, successful and thoroughly enjoying path. Finances are better. I'm back on my feet and loving life! I've hit rock bottom in so many ways....got pummeled down there....but somehow, I never gave up hope. I fought to get back up. I got knocked down again and again but FUCK that! I never stopped my laughter amidst so many tears. I didn't allow the negativity that surrounded me the past four plus years to quell my optimistic attitude towards life. I am far from fucking perfect...I've proved that many times over. But, I love who I am and I love where I am in life. It took a lot to get here and I'm proud of all I've accomplished.

My parents ended up getting divorced. I truly believe their reaction towards my cancer was a direct reflection based on their own issues. Nothing I could have possibly done can/could ever warrant a parent from dumping their child during the most difficult time of her life. You have cancer? Well, I'll make your life even more miserable. Breast cancer didn't kill you off yet? Don't worry – we'll make your life so miserable that the stress alone will. That's NOT how it's fucking supposed to work!

The great news is that my dad apologized to me. Did he do this on his own volition? No. His amazing girlfriend was behind it. Mama Andrea could not believe even his version (we all know each person has their own favorable version of what really happened). She said, "This is YOUR DAUGHTER! How dare you! You need to apologize to your daughter. Nothing, ABSOLUTELY NOTHING she could have done warrants this type of behavior!"

Finally. Thank you Mama Andrea!

Someone was able to knock some sense into at least one of my parents.

We had tried, unsuccessfully, over the years to all reconcile, but it didn't work. I NEEDED acknowledgment, along with an apology, to be able to forge ahead. A simple, "I was wrong and I'm sorry" would have sufficed. No explanations were needed. Just a basic acknowledgment and a simple apology would have gotten things moving along. I recognize that apologies are never easy, nor is admitting you are wrong, but it was necessary for my healing to begin.

Instead, all I got were excuses. Fingers pointing blame. They all blamed my pain meds, which I hardly took because of their ridiculous accusations. My surgeons were upset with me because they knew the crazy pain I was in and knew I needed those pain meds. I was an amputee, for fuck's sake! Who gets body parts amputated and refuses pain meds? Me. Sadly. Stupidly. So fuckingly stupid. They blamed anything and everything they could to justify their abandoning me at the WORST fucking time of my life. The sad thing is, they not only abandoned me, but they abandoned my kids. They destroyed the sense of "family" we all thought we had. Difficult times like these are supposed to bring families together. In my situation, I found myself all alone.

My mom still hasn't acknowledged nor apologized. I learned a lot about my family over those four years. My family was NOT the way I had always thought they were. What a HUGE fucking disappointment to discover that. Some people always play the victim. I won't. I refuse. I learned and I move forward. I'm strong. I stood alone for years. I can do ANY FUCKING THING I need to and I don't need to rely on anyone. What a fucked up way to learn a lesson.

I still love my parents. I still love my brother. I despise my sister, that's never changed. My dad and I have more of a relationship now thanks to his beautifully hearted and well-grounded girlfriend. My mom and I are working on a relationship despite hardly seeing each other. Then again, she does live in Florida. Do I believe they still love me? Yes. I'm their first born, the free spirited child they tried to control and contain but after forty plus years they finally realized they never could. I'm their own flesh and blood, unless someone's not telling me something! My brother and I are cordial when we see each other, but we don't have the relationship I once thought we had nor will we ever.

Do we need to automatically love someone because we are related? I didn't choose my family unlike what my mother always told me. I was born into this family and had to make my way. I always felt my mother loved my sister more than me. I learned this was true that very day she abandoned me (breast cancer patient) to care for my sister (NOT a cancer patient at all, just stressed over the fact that I was getting unwanted attention because of course who the fuck wants cancer?!!). Who had the cancer? Hmmmmm. Who was a single mom with no help? Hmmmmmmm.

They always say, in your greatest times of need, you will find out who truly loves you and who doesn't. Don't be shocked when those closest to you are the first to run. It's a shocking thought, yes. But, it's a sad reality. You may feel alone, like I did. But, you're not. I'm right with ya. It happens to many of us. I'm not sure many had their parents WANT to arrest them, too, but shit, it makes for a good story years later!

I had friends and local acquaintances coordinate meals for weeks after my double mastectomy. I don't think I ever had that much food in my fridge, never mind in my house, at one time. I had visits. I had love and support from those

I expected to get it from and those I never expected. I could never thank those people enough.

Perceptions of family were delusions but now that reality hit me over the head, I'm ok with where things are at. Disappointing? Absofuckinlutely. The good thing is that my kids are aware of everything now that they are old enough to really understand. My kids know I will ALWAYS be there for them. I don't care what they could ever do, I will always love them and support them. I would give them my last breath, my last cent, my last everything.

I love my mom. I love my dad. I love my brother. I'll say it all again. Do I truly respect them for what they did to me? No. Are we working towards a better relationship because life is short? Yes. Am I doing this in great part for my kids so they have a newfound sense of family? Absofuckinlutely. Have I missed what I thought I always had? Yes. But, I learned that it wasn't real and I'll never have that again.

Chapter Fucking 17
Menopause

How many women are grateful for menopause? I sure as fuck am! I reached menopause on my very own without any Tamoxifen. I'm praying this helps diminish my chances for the cancer returning, and my body cooperated all on its very own!!

Has menopause affected my sex life? Noooo way! Has it affected my wallet? Sure – no more tampons or maxi pads. Has it affected my chin? OMG yes….watch out for those long unwanted hairs that randomly pop up, two freakin' inches long that you didn't see when you went to bed and shockingly find when you wake up in the morning! Daily close inspections are VITAL and the need for strategically placed tweezers is crucial. I suppose it helps that I don't have nipples given no hair can grow around there as I'm told happens to some women. One of the "perks" of losing your real breasts I suppose!

Hot flashes – oh my lord! Hot like a mother fucker! I'm the only one sweating while walking the frigid streets of New York City in 28 degree weather. I'm the one fanning myself with sweat dripping down my boobs and my back. I'm the one kicking the covers off in the middle of the night not just once, not just twice, but all fucking night, waking my boyfriend each and every time. As soon as those hot flashes come on, they disappear and I'm back to normal.

Ladies, even if you need Tamoxifen and you are forced into early menopause, it's really ok. If Tamoxifen is in your best interest, you can deal with early menopause. It's really not that bad!

Tamoxifen isn't for everyone. Please make sure you get a second opinion as I did if you have any doubts.

Chapter Fucking 18
Boobless in Mexico

I was craving a vacation yet I had very little money. I found a cheap all-inclusive trip to Cancun, Mexico, and decided to bring my kids. My son didn't want to go. My daughter did. So, I had her invite a friend. Her friend and her friend's Mom, who is also a friend of mine, elected to join us. We pretended we were family and shared a room together on the beach in a three star hotel. Don't forget, I was on a very tight budget! It was a WONDERFUL vacation.

The tough part for me was that I had no breasts at the time. My first set of implants had just been removed and I was flat as a boy. I went to a local discount store called Ocean State Job Lot for $10 bathing suits, knowing they were just for this occasion. I tried to find padded bikini tops that would disguise all the folds of excess skin I had while trying to make me feel somewhat feminine and normal. I was mortified, walking around with no breasts. I was embarrassed. But wait, WHO THE FUCK KNEW I HAD NO BREASTS?! I could have been normally flat chested for all anyone knew. But I knew. And I had a very difficult time with it.

Walking through the airport scans were a hoot. In place of my breast prosthetics, I used those pads found in padded bathing suits to add a little bump in my flat chest. The problem was, they weren't placed properly. I recall walking through and being pulled aside for a pat down. Now, I hadn't been "pat down" in quite some time so I was looking forward to it! Joke, of course! I turned to look at the picture taken from the scan and started cracking up. My "boobs" (those "pads") looked ridiculous on the scan – no wonder why they wanted to pat me down. I was crying of laughter and explained, "I just want boobs! I just want boobs!"

I had gotten two sets of breast prosthetics. One pair was designed for everyday use, another good for water/swimming. I got them just in time for our trip but after attempting to wear them a few times, I HATED them. I had "boobs" with them, but the bra I had to fit them into was less than desirable given I had to wear closed neck shirts so the bra wouldn't be seen, it was large and the prosthetics were very heavy.

Here's a fucking funny story for you! The day I picked up my prosthetics, I showed my kids. We were sitting around the kitchen table and my kids were playing with the prosthetics. It was quite a novelty! After a while, I said, "How does it feel to be playing with my boobs?!" OMG was I cracking up! They tossed the boobs up in the air in disgust when they realized that in fact, they WERE playing with my boobs!!! My fake boobs, of course.

I refused to bring the bulky uncomfortable prosthetics on the trip. I went boobless and I still felt beautiful.

I had a fabulous time, a well needed and deserved vacation. Inexpensive yet tons of fun.

Chapter Fucking 19
Tattoos, Boobs and My Masterpiece

When I first had my double mastectomy, my plan was to either get nipples surgically constructed and tattooed or 3-D nipple tattoos. Unfortunately, I was butchered by the bitchy butcher plastic surgeon and that couldn't happen for quite some time. After eight major breast surgeries (don't forget – 6 were corrective reconstructive by my GOOD plastic surgeon!), I decided it was too late for nipples in any form. My new fantabulous plastic surgeon, Dr. Mark, could only do so much with the disaster he was presented with. And, he did an amazing job, all considering.

Every time I looked in the mirror, I cried. There was a time I was crying every fucking day. It wasn't just the visual that I got when seeing my breasts in the mirror. It was what those breasts signified to me. They signified loss. Lots of fucking loss.

I lost my breasts.
I lost my family or at least what I thought I had with regards to "family".
I lost my son for a year.
I lost my business.
I lost a lot of money.
I lost a lot of time.

I did a lot of research on line. I saw some pictures of breast cancer survivors with tattoos splayed across their chests. I delved into this deeper and decided, "That's it! That's what I'm going to do when I'm all done!" I started looking for designs I would love to incorporate into my "masterpiece". My last breast surgery was early Spring of 2018. On my 48th birthday, I took the day off and went to see a tattoo artist for the initial session.

My Masterpiece had begun!

I will first tell you about this tattoo artist. He was an acquaintance of mine who knew of my journey. He had a rough exterior and the kindest heart, a long time tattoo artist who offered to tattoo my breasts as a gift. This was to be the last stop in my breast cancer journey. This gift is a gift that keeps me smiling every time I look at myself in the mirror. This is a gift that encourages others to do the same, to find peace, to make something beautiful out of something so horrible.

The tattoo began. I had numerous sessions with this tattoo artist. Each and every
time, the tattoo took on a new life of its own. It blossomed and evolved into the magnificent masterpiece it is today. He squeezed me in between appointments, he never charged me a penny and he realized the importance of his work and how it can make such a huge impact on a mutilated survivor such as myself. He decided to close his shop at the end of December, 2018. A few months later, he decided to re-open elsewhere with a new focus –

tattooing over scars. In so graciously helping me, he changed the course of his career. He has re-invented himself and has found new purpose for his amazing gifts. I'm so happy to know he can do this for other people as well.

I have a beautiful bouquet of roses cascading all over my breasts. Every time I look at them, I smile. No more tears. Wait, I shouldn't say that. There will always be some tears but not the way they used to be. I LOVE my ink. I LOVE showing it off. I worked so hard for it and I'm so proud of it. I LOVE when I get a shocking double take from people given I don't look the "type" to have tattoos. I LOVE dispelling the stereotypes people place on those with tattoos. In my mind, my tattoos are a sign of my fucking SURVIVAL. Outside of birthing my two beautiful children, my survival is one of the best fucking accomplishments I've ever made. And, I'm damn fucking proud!!!

Chapter Fucking 20
The "PERKS" Of Perky Fuckers

Let's look at the positive!

Ok, yeah, it fucking sucks that breast cancer took my real breasts. I fucking LOVED those things. They were double D's, sometimes triple D's....awesome cleavage....filled every top and dress so fucking beautifully....great sex appeal....so feminine...and...beautiful large suckable nipples!!!

I'm a huge proponent on looking at the "perks" of a situation.

Let's begin!

*Perky Fuckers Forever. These puppies will NEVER sag!
*I can wear ANYTHING I want without worrying about which bra to wear or whether or not I have to wear one.
*No erect nipples embarrassingly protruding through my clothes although I do find that rather sexy....
*No use for nipple clamps (LMAO!!!)
*(Damn, I miss my nipples....but keeping this perky and positive....)
*Living in a retirement home at the ripe old age of 95 and still having the perkiest sexiest gravity defying boobs in the joint!
*Shocking medical professionals at EVERY fucking doctor appointment with my tattooed boobs. Priceless!

*Pulling an "Arnold" move and flexing your boobs to music is quite a new talent!!
*Synchronizing your "boob flex" with your "arm flex"....talk about a strange feeling but pretty fucking cool!
*NO BLACK EYES! You won't hit yourself in the face when you run...or even walk...great safety feature.
*No more mammograms for those who hate them. I never minded them but no more boobs = no more squishy painful pancakes!
*NO MORE LEAKY TITS!!!

Chapter Fucking 21
Boob Photo Shoot and Painting Party

There was so much to get done between the day I was diagnosed to the day of my double mastectomy. I arranged for coverage at the salon I owned, had numerous pre-op medical appointments, half assly celebrated my 45th birthday somewhere in there amongst the fucking sadness and tears, made arrangements for the kids and the dogs, devised a will with my attorney so that my kids would be protected in every way possible, bought the necessary items for post-surgical comfort and last but not least, made time for a professional photo shoot of my breasts.

I'm sure that sounds crazy to most, but I wanted to "preserve" my original breasts in the only way I knew. This amazing photographer didn't charge me a penny for the photoshoot. The photo shoot was a bittersweet moment for me. I didn't feel beautiful at the time. I felt sad and depressed. But, the pictures came out absolutely stunning!

My plan was to hang up a "before" boob shot and an "after" boob shot in my own bedroom. Why? I'll tell you the fuck why. Survival. That's fucking why! My original breasts began my journey and the tatted up finished product ended it. And, throughout it all, I survived. I'm still the fuck here. I miss my old breasts - they FAILED me.

They nurtured both of my children but they fucking flat assed failed me.

Sitting in the bleachers one afternoon, after my double mastectomy, while watching my daughter cheer, I had a wild fucking idea. One of the other mothers had a side business and painted kids' faces at parties. I thought, heck, why not paint my boobs! So, I asked her and she loved the idea. I had around 10 female friends over for this unconventional party. It was so fucking therapeutic! Yes, I'm an odd one but it was a wonderful way to promote my own healing and a wonderful way for my friends to show their love and support. We laughed...a whole fucking lot!! I walked around topless, with painted boobs. We ate boob themed food. We drank wine from pink bottles. We made boob themed drinks such as slippery nipple. And we fucking laughed some more.

Life is meant to be enjoyed, people. So, enjoy it! Make the most of it. Life serves you lemons, you fucking make a lemon chiffon pie!! Try and find that which makes you happy. No matter how fucking difficult things seem, there is always a reason to smile…..which leads me to my next chapter…..

Chapter Fucking 22
Smile, Support & Counseling

Smile!

No matter what is going on in your fucked up life, there is ALWAYS a reason to smile. If you can't see the reason, MAKE the fucking reason.

Getting told I had breast cancer did NOT make me fucking smile. In fact, it brought me into a situational type of depression. But, did I find reason to smile? You sure as heck bet your skinny little fucking ass I did! Side note, I wish I had a skinny little fucking ass....lol!

I was miserable...crying all the time. So miserable that the mother of one of my daughter's friends found me a support group to go to. I figured why the fuck not. I showed up early for the meeting because I was so nervous (for those of you that know me well, tardiness or being fashionably late was more my speed). I don't go to support meetings! I don't need help! What the fuck?!

Two people arrived before me. All of a sudden, this wonderful man named Bob approached me and thrust his hand out for a welcoming hand shake. This is how it went down...

Bob: "Hello! I'm Bob. Breast cancer survivor. Single mastectomy. And I'm gay."

Me: "Hi Bob. I'm Cindy. Breast cancer survivor. Double mastectomy. And I'm straight. Nice to meet you!"

He was the only man in attendance and that very day, I learned something interesting. Breast cancer affects BOTH genders! Who the fuck knew?! Men can get mammos. Men can get mastectomies. Approximately one in 833 men get breast cancer and sadly, because men aren't "supposed" to get breast cancer, it is often caught in later stages. Crazy!!

Side note and worthy of mentioning...Bob has gone on to raise awareness that men can get breast cancer. Bob was diagnosed in May of 2012, at the age of 49, with stage 3A male breast cancer. In June of 2012, he had a single mastectomy, followed by six rounds of chemo and 25 rounds of radiation. He is on a 10-year course of Tamoxifen and in fact, coincidentally, uses the same amazeballs breast surgeon that I do, Dr. Beth Sieling. Unfortunately, he was recently diagnosed with early stage prostate cancer but his doctors are closely monitoring him. Bob is a fucking survivor! Go Bob!

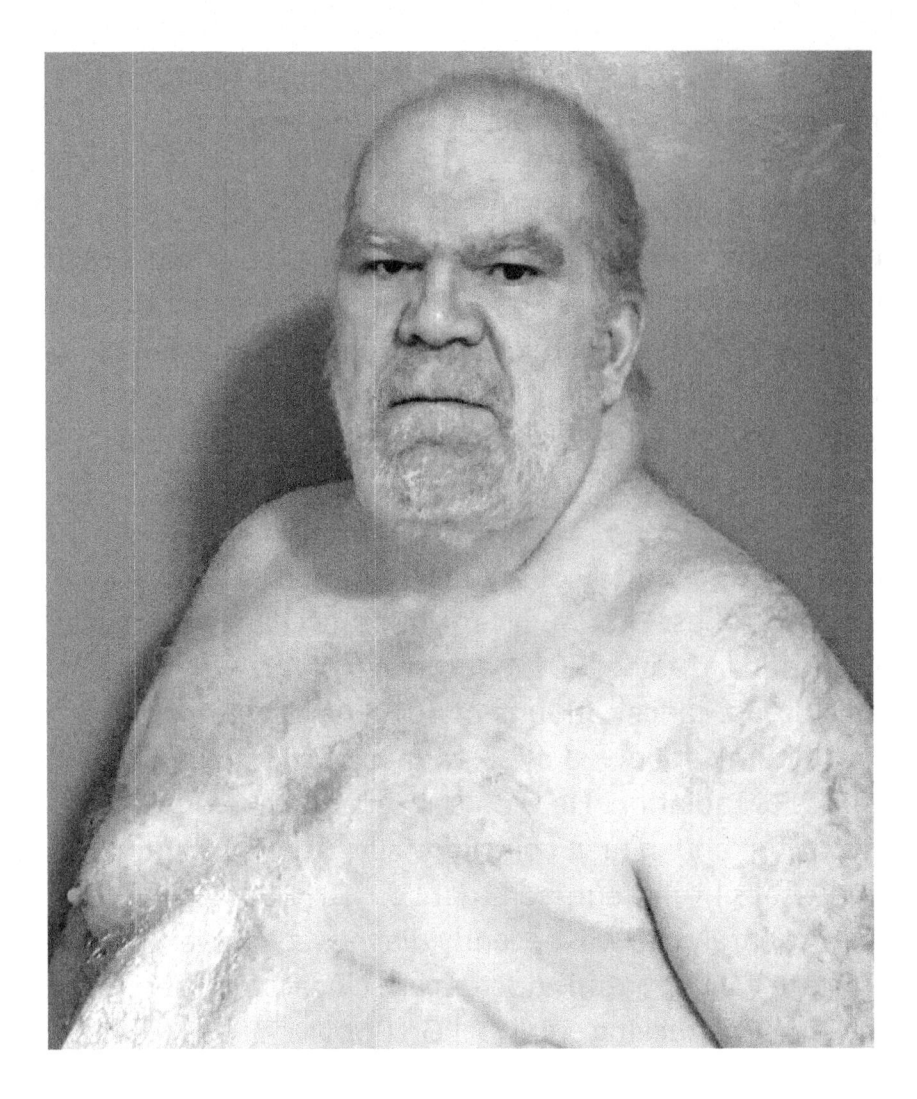

Pictured is my friend Bob. Single mastectomy male breast cancer survivor Bob. He is one brave warrior!

The meeting was beneficial in many ways. I only went to a couple more after that. In each meeting, many bared their boobs for others to see (Bob so graciously turned around out of respect), sharing their own personal experiences and journeys – different surgeries, different surgeons, different issues, etc. And you know the fuck what? It gave me a little peace of mind knowing that I wasn't alone. It helped give me an idea as to what to expect. I didn't really "click" with the group as a whole, nor am I cut out for group therapy sessions, but it was filled with lovely supportive women and Bob, of course.

I decided to find a counselor. Kelly. She was amazing! She looked like a young Barbie doll, so tiny, perfectly beautiful, so sweet and so fucking kind. It was hysterical when she said the word, "Fuck"! She was a real fucking person who understood all I was going through. At one point during my counseling sessions, I asked her point blank, "Am I crazy?" I reminded her that she's paid to be honest so she better just say it like it is.

Kelly's response, "You're not crazy. You're colorful!" Now, I LIKE colorful! Kelly couldn't believe all I had been through and all I continued to go through. Fucking family shit, cancer shit, business shit, biker shit, you name it!

Kelly told me something I'll never forget, "Cindy, do you realize that no matter how sad you are, you always find something to smile and laugh about? Even amidst your tears? You'll be ok. You need to cry when you feel it but don't let it consume you. Keep finding reasons to laugh. I applaud you because most people would allow their circumstances to destroy them and their happiness. You don't. You are an inspiration."

One day, after leaving her office, I passed by her next client. This client was a teenager, suicidal and schizophrenic. I learned all this from talking to her Mom a few times in the waiting room. This young lady said to me, "I could hear your laugh and it made me feel so good, so peaceful. I couldn't hear what you said, but I could hear your laugh and I loved it."

So find a fucking reason to laugh! Find a fucking reason to smile! It will make YOU feel better as well as all those around you.

Kelly saw me for a couple of years. She watched me go through all the emotions. She saw me cope. I coped well, all considering! I didn't allow myself to self destroy. I fucking coped. She understood me. She supported me. I will forever be grateful to Kelly for all she did to help me navigate this god awful journey I found myself on.

As I've mentioned before, the journey sucked but the destination is amazing. Never forget, things happen the way they are fucking meant to. It doesn't mean it's enjoyable and it doesn't mean we will ever understand the reasons, but your life will unfold as it was destined to. Trust in the journey.

Don't let this sweet face fool you! Kelly is an amazing therapist with a huge heart, but she's tougher than she looks. I used to call her "Barbie" because she's absolutely perfect, beautiful on the outside and beautiful on the inside. I credit this woman for helping me heal, for understanding my plight, for giving me guidance, support and strength as I navigated through years of unknowns, fear and sadness. Kelly holds a special place in my heart. If you are ever in need of counseling with one of the best therapists out there, call Kelly Fortin, LPC of The Center for Emotional Healing, LLC. You're welcome. You'll thank me later! Guaranteed!

Chapter Fucking 23
Cry

Cry – it's ok! Crying is a form of release.

No one receiving news like I did laughs in the face of a death sentence. Well, no normal fucker would and that's not saying I'm normal by any stretch of anyone's fucked up imagination!

I cried a lot. I sat in my breast surgeon, Dr. Beth Sieling's office that horrible day, May 15th, 2015. As soon as I heard the news, the tears started to pour out of my eyes and down my cheeks. Those fucking tears lasted four fucking years!

I cried non-stop for years. Some find it hard to believe, that this positive happy person could cry so much. I still cry but not as often as I once did. I found crying in the shower was the best place to cry although the tears didn't always stop there. Kelly, my counselor, told me it's ok to cry, every day if need be, but once it's done, keep moving the fuck forward.

There were times I sunk to my shower floor, curled up in a ball, feeling so fucking defeated and alone, crying from the depths of my soul. I made sure that no one was home when that happened. I know if I heard that come out of someone I loved, I would be heartbroken and never forget the haunting sound of their pain. I didn't want to scar my children any more than they already were. But, it HAD to come out and I found the shower was the best place for that. Alone. Alone with my fucking thoughts. Water cascading all over my body. Tears escaping my eyes and washed away by the shower. I'd always pick myself up, finish up my shower and start my day.

The tears lessened after the first year and a half, for a bit, but increased soon after. Every fucking day I cried. How could I emotionally seem to get better and then take a turn for the worse? I fucking survived! Why the fuck did I cry every fucking day? Who the fuck knows. All I know is that we all deal differently. Every time I saw my breasts OR thought about something having to do with the breast cancer (and that includes all the loss I endured during that time), I fucking cried. Every time I looked at my breasts, I cried.

Somehow, the tears became less and less. Somehow, as time went on, I must have accepted my fate in life because you know what? You need to just fucking accept the shit. Life happens and you need to continue to move forward. The alternative is that you're stuck, you're miserable, you're sad and no one wants to be around a fucker like that. Even more importantly, you don't like yourself. You can never find happiness if you're stuck in a bad place in your fucked up head.

Bad shit happens to good people all the fucking time. Does that make any fucking sense? NO! But, here's my quote, "It is what it FUCKING is!" So, suck it up buttercups and deal. People often like to justify why shit happens to us good people but you know what? There's NO fucking justification for it!

Some crazy fuckers even tell me, "I'm glad I had cancer!" WHAT THE FUCK?! Seriously? You're glad you were given a fucking death sentence? You're glad you went through all that misery? No, you're not. Don't fucking lie! Truth is that we learn so much about those around us as we navigate this awful path. We learn a lot about ourselves, too. But, is this really the way you want to learn? I believe not.

So cry it out! Stock up on those soft lotion infused tissues and a lot of ointment for your red chaffed nose and let it out. Crying is a wonderful release. Man, woman, masculine, feminine….it really doesn't matter. We are ALL entitled to cry. But, don't let it consume you. When it starts to take over, that's when you need help. Reach out to loved ones, family, friends, support groups, counselors, psychiatrists and if you need meds, even temporarily, it's really OK! You need to do WHATEVER you need to do to get through this. It can break you but you can't let it.

I recall a song coming on the radio that inspired me. Every fucking time I heard it, it empowered me and encouraged me to KEEP FIGHTING!!! There were times I needed to listen to it and other times it "coincidentally" came out on the radio when I needed to hear it (although I don't believe in coincidences – I believe in synchronicity).

So just listen to me and listen good or I'll fuck you up. Kidding. I won't fuck you up (unless you give me reason to). But, listen to me, because this is so important for your healing. Cry. It's really fucking ok. I still cry.

Chapter Fucking 24
Why Me??

Fuck.
Cancer.
My fucking life.
Changed.
Boobs.
Gone.
Family.
Joke. Family?!
Fuck 'em.
Fears.
Forever.
Smile.
My Façade.
Tears.
Lurk behind my eyes.
Alone.
I cry. I can't help it.
Pain.
Physical. Emotional.
Alone.
Time to think.
Time to mourn.
Time to cry.
Let down my cheerful façade.
Collapse.
Body curled up.
Wet cheeks. Salty.

Swollen eyes.
Questions.
Why me????????

Chapter Fucking 25
I Fucking WIN!

Cancer.
Sucks.
Four years of challenges.
I survived!
Family walked.
Blamed my cancer.
Blamed the anaesthesia.
Blamed pain meds.
Bu-bye controlling assholes.
Bu-bye manipulators.
Bu-bye abusers.
Strength.
Fucking strength.
Survival – yes, I survived.
Love.
Friends.
Support.
"Family" is chosen.
Forge ahead.
Cope.
Cry less.
Laugh more.
But still cry.
Spread awareness.
Find humor.
Laugh.
Love.

Make love.
Live.
Passion.
Hug.
Compassion.
Reach out and help others.
New FUCKING BOOBIES.
Tattoos.
Fucking DONE!
No.
Never done.
Breast cancer survivor.
True warrior.
Battles fought far beyond cancer.
Truth.
Happiness.
Health.
Gratitude.
FUCK YOU CANCER.
I FUCKING WIN!!!

Chapter Fucking 26
YOU Are Fucking BEAUTIFUL!

Perfection.

Fucking perfection.

YOU.

Yes, you.

You are fucking beautiful.

Society has a fucked up way of making us feel "less than". Fuck that! We are ALL beautiful. Fat, thin, tall, short, bald, long hair, short hair, blue eyes, brown eyes, old, young, wrinkles, scars, who the fuck cares?! There is beauty in each and every single one of us.

Sadly, many of us who have mastectomies suffer from poor self-image, poor self-esteem. We feel "incomplete" without our breasts. We feel "less than" a woman because we are missing that which we feel makes us feminine. I totally get that. I was the same! We identify with our breasts. Then, we are faced with losing them and it's devastating.

I can honestly say my two favorite features were my hair and my breasts. How fucking ironic that I was faced with losing BOTH. I lost my breasts, yes. Out of all the choices I was given, the double mastectomy was the most aggressive and Dr. Beth Sieling's top choice. I loved my breasts and she knew it. Beth knew it was a hard decision for me. I took the weekend to ponder all the info she had given me but in my heart of hearts, I knew what I had to do.

The absolute worst was seeing myself without any breasts and tons of excess sucked in skin. I recall the night I spent in the hospital after my first fucked up set of torpedo like gummy bear implants were removed by my top notch plastic surgeon, Dr. Mark. I got out of the hospital bed to use the bathroom. I decided to take a peek at my flat chest and see what I looked like. I unwrapped my top and screamed. I was in absolute shock! What the fuck happened to me! Why do I look like this? I had drains on each side of where my breasts should have been and all this absolutely disgusting looking skin that was being sucked into my chest in odd places because of the drains.

My chest looked like silly putty that was squeezed and flattened and folded over and over and over again. Just then, the nurse came into my room and saw me having a mental breakdown in my bathroom. She ran over to me and I turned to her, wide eyed and topless, pointing to my chest and asked her what the fuck happened to me! Why do I look like this! The nurse had never seen anything like it. I could see the fear in her eyes. She had no clue why I looked the way I did yet tried to cover the shock that overcame her. She tried to calm me down and told me to go lay back down while she called the plastic surgeon.

My amazing plastic surgeon, Dr. Mark, immediately called her back. She ran back into my room with the phone. He understood how scared I was and explained why I had to look like that for a few months. Body image. FUCK. I was not only flat chested but it was fucking scary looking! It wasn't his fault, it was just a necessary evil to prevent me from going toxic from the bitchy butcher's errors and to begin the corrective reconstructive process. But imagine how ugly I felt! To this day, when I look at my pictures and see those in particular, I still cry.

I WISH I didn't feel so ugly at that time. Cancer is ugly enough. It leaves it's marks on us. It scars our outsides. It's scarred my insides, too. But I'm a strong mother fucking woman and you know the fuck what? I'm still beautiful. Flaws, scars, boobs, no boobs, chunk, junk in the trunk, wrinkles and all!

As I previously mentioned, I used to own a tanning salon and a boutique. Every time I'd spray tan a woman, I would hear excuses for what they perceived as "flaws". It hurt my fucking heart to hear all these women make excuses for their beautiful bodies! NO ONE IS PERFECT. And, truly, who the fuck decides what IS perfect?!

It really bothered me so I wrote the following article. I hung a copy in each and every tanning room in my salon. I had women come to me crying, thanking me. I had women commend me for stating something so inspiring. I had women with scars and eating disorders and body image issues thank me for empowering them, even if for just that moment.

So, please read....and feel empowered. Always remember, YOU ARE PERFECT JUST AS YOU ARE. BOOBS, NO BOOBS, NIPPLES, NO NIPPLES. PERFECTION. OWN IT, GIRL!!!

Bodies are Beautiful

Bodies are my palette. I don't see flaws. I see beauty when I see a bare skin body in my shop. Male/female, old/young, heavy/thin, tall/short, dark/light, tattoos/piercings...it's a body before me and I approach it as an artist, ready to apply my finishing touches.

Years ago, when I was at my thinnest, I recall being on the beach with my first child. A news reporter was roaming the beach asking thin patrons this particular question..."should heavy women wear bikinis?" Why would this be newsworthy??! I tried to reach out to the reporter but wasn't able to catch him in time. Despite being thin at the time, my weight had been a constant struggle over the years and continues to be. I wanted to tell him I was in a bikini when I was heavy. I was in a bikini when I was pregnant. I was in a bikini at that very moment. And, most importantly, I wanted to tell him that EVERYONE is beautiful!

Fast forward to today. I own a tanning salon and boutique where I offer hand held organic spray tans to women of all ages and sizes. Two years ago, I never would have thought I'd be in the business. Two years ago, I never envisioned myself an artist who would work with the human body. Two years ago, I never thought I'd make such a positive impact on someone's self-esteem by helping to make them feel good about themselves. Two years ago, I felt the same way about bodies as I do today but my spray tanning experiences have only solidified my beliefs.

Most women I spray tan are timid at first, trying to hide their bodies from me or making excuses for their perceived imperfections. Society unfairly imposes the notion of "perfection". During the course of the past two years, I can safely say that I've seen hundreds and hundreds of bare skin bodies. I have seen every single angle possible of every single body before me. The markings on our bodies that some may perceive as flaws, in fact, tell a story...our own individual story. Strength, survival, whatever your story...it's yours and one you should be proud of.

One of the many incidents that warmed my heart was when one young nervous woman stopped me during the spray tan application to tell me something. I was concerned and asked her if she was ok. Her response, "I just have to tell you...you have made me feel so comfortable! Thank you!"

Recently, songs are promoting positive body image. It's about time! Models come in all sizes now. Finally! Out of all the bodies I have spray tanned, I can confidently report that the norm is NOT anorexic as portrayed in the media! I am now considered an expert in my field so listen as I tell you something very important. And, please spread the word......

What is perfect? I'll tell you what is perfect. You. You are perfect. You are perfect just as you are.

Chapter Fucking 27
Me, A Fucking Calendar Girl

I decided to try out to be in a calendar. Yes, me.

This calendar used real, everyday women, of all ages, of all sizes, of all backgrounds. I thought to myself, "Self, want to be in a calendar?" My response, "Sure, why the fuck not!" So, I tried out and guess the fuck what?! You guessed it. I became Miss June 2019.

The day of tryouts, I cried all fucking day. It was a bad day for me. I was miserable. Depressed. I stayed in bed the whole day feeling sorry for myself. I almost blew off the tryouts but something in me made me get up. I showered. I dressed. I put in my contacts and a little make up on my face. My eyes were puffy, red and swollen but heck, "It is what it fucking is". I made the hour long drive to Hartford, Connecticut, and almost drove right past the house, purposely. Something made me stop, park and go inside. I brought my article along, "Bodies are Beautiful".

I interviewed with four or five women, had a lovely time and felt that just being there was a huge fucking accomplishment for myself regardless of whether I was chosen or not. I pushed myself out of my comfort zone and forced myself to break free of my misery and depression for a short time.

Shortly after, I discovered I was chosen to be one of the calendar girls. How exciting! I made a commitment, formed a new type of sisterhood with all of the women involved in the making of the calendar and began to shop for 50's style pin up clothing. I fucking love to shop so of course, I ended up spending far too much money on the dresses, shoes and accessories than I should have. Contracts were signed and the fun began.

My photo shoot was at this eclectic artsy fartsy place that sadly, ended up closing. It was a colorful place, filled with colorful things and colorful people. It looked like a carnival on the outside. My hair and make-up helped create the 50's pin up look and the photo shoot was so much fun.

Karen Stanford, a dear friend, a fellow biker, a beautiful woman with a beautiful soul, founded Connecticut Calendar Girlz as a means to raise money and awareness to the issue of domestic violence. All of the proceeds went to organizations in Connecticut that helped victims of domestic violence. She took so much time out of her life to put this calendar together every year and it was quite an honor to be a part.

Many of the women in this calendar had life stories of their own to share and many were not good stories. I have not yet mentioned my own experiences with domestic violence. Suffice it to say, I had a fucking miserable ex-husband who did some horrible things to me. Surgery corrected some of it but I was considered a battered wife for many years. I decided to divorce his ugly ass to make sure my kids understood that the fucked up relationship they witnessed was not the norm. Thankfully, it worked.

This calendar was another of my accomplishments, one in which I never imagined. I attended all sorts of car and bike shows, sold calendars and other support items and helped raise over $16,000 that year through our efforts. It was truly a memorable experience and one I will forever treasure.

Moral of this chapter – step out of your fucking way, step out of your fucking comfort zone, try new things, force yourself when you need to, don't let yourself drown in self misery, take one step at a time, one day at a time, one moment at a time and you will slowly heal. Healing is a process so have patience with yourself. You WILL heal. It may happen at a slow ass turtle's pace but it'll fucking happen.

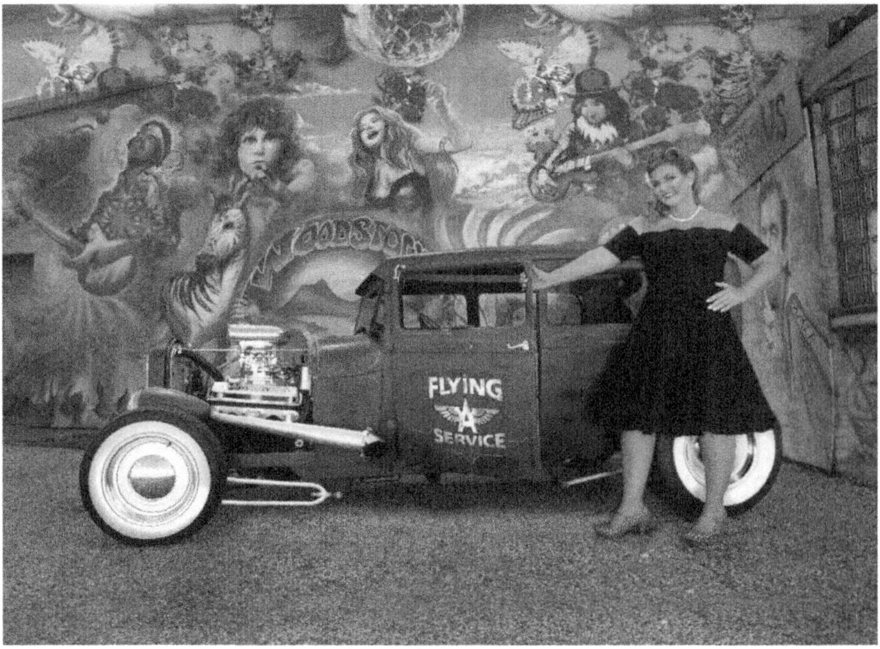
FLYING
A
SERVICE

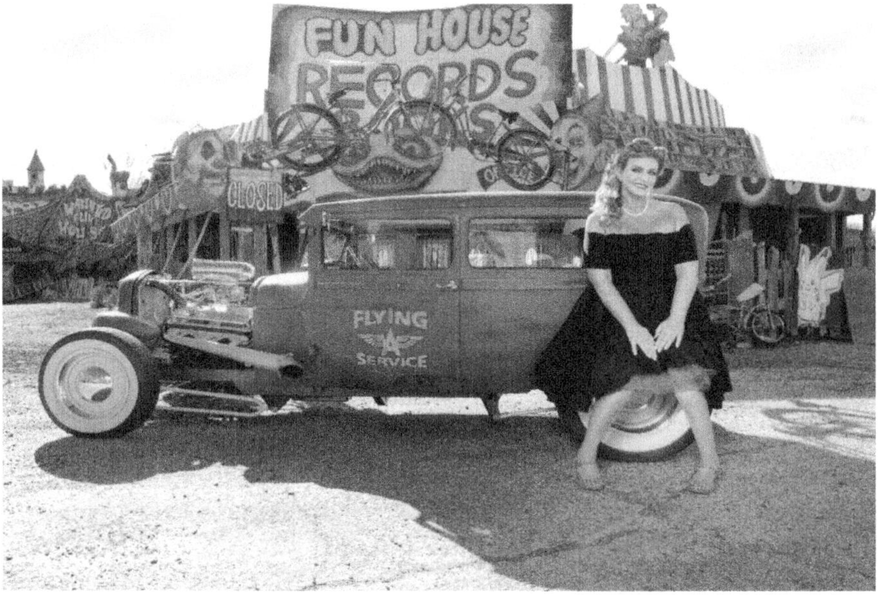
FUN HOUSE
RECORDS
CLOSED
FLYING
A
SERVICE

All Connecticut Calendar Girlz photos by the beautiful Karen Stanford.

Chapter Fucking 28
Why Does Bad Shit Happen To Good People?

Seriously, why does bad shit always happen to good people?

I have always been a fucking law abiding citizen. I pay my taxes, I have never stolen, I stop to help random strangers stuck on the side of the road (the elderly, women and kids), I always stop and help animals hit in the middle of the road (fucking stupid at times I know, especially when it's a rattlesnake or a 200 lb snapping turtle!), I don't leave a mess behind in the department stores like some people I know, I thank people for good service and often put it in writing and give to upper management in the hopes they will get recognized for the wonderful service they provide, I take in rescue dogs, I spend my last cent on caring for all those I love, I give even if I don't have, yet I FUCKING GET CANCER. What the FUCK is wrong with this picture?!

I fucking cried more in the past four and a half years than I've cried in 49 years. For fucks sake, and as a random example, why is it that some nasty wench out to destroy people's lives can live forever without any serious ailments yet a warm hearted peace loving woman, such as myself, of course, is forced to endure such pain, trials, tribulations and loss?

I was on social media at the time and decided to change my last name. Now, this is funny shit or at least I think so. I wanted to be, "Cindy Boobaliscious". Well, it wouldn't allow me to use that last name. Why the fuck not? What if I really changed my name to Boobaliscious? So, I tried, "Cindy Boobaluscious". That didn't work either. What the fuck?! I couldn't be Cindy Sevell, my married and now divorced name, nor could I be Cindy Knepler, my maiden pre-marriage and pre-divorced name. I decided I needed my own fucking identity and I needed to lose my last name. I needed to be JUST ME. So, I went with my first and middle names. Cindy Leah. Lib-the-fuck-erating! I couldn't stand my family. I couldn't stand my ex-husband. I didn't want to belong to anyone who was out to fucking destroy me or kick me when I'm down.

I took steps to try and understand, empower myself, better myself given my situation. Sadly, there are just things we will never understand, such as, "Why does bad shit happen to good people?!" All we have to do is keep plugging away. There are things we can't stop or prevent, but we can keep our head up, not accept this as our doomed destiny and keep fucking fighting! We all get dealt a bad hand at some point in our lives. Some have it worse than others and there is no fucking explanation that makes any sense as to why any of us need to suffer BUT, as the title of my book states, "It is what it FUCKING is!"

When you think you have it bad, look around you. Sure, your shit sucks but there are others with some stinkier ass shit that makes you feel blessed for the lower level of shit you do have. The other day, I was sitting at a restaurant with my daughter and a young man walked by with severe physical handicaps. My heart went out to him and I thought to myself, "My shit sucked smelly ass but it's over. He has to live with his shit on a daily basis for the rest of his life."

Pick yourself up, dust yourself off, pull up your big girl panties (but be careful not to give yourself one of those vajayjay wedgies – those fucking hurt) and say to yourself, "I fucking got this shit! It stinks but IT IS WHAT IT FUCKING IS!!!"

Chapter Fucking 29
Boob Shots – Professional Before and After Shots

I mentioned earlier that I wanted to preserve and memorialize my boobs. How the fuck do you do this? Cut them off and stick them in a jar full of formaldehyde? Stick the jar on your kitchen counter and display your tits? Make molds out of your boobs and create some fantabulous sculptures to decorate your house? Wait a hot fucking minute – I wish I thought of that one sooner! I would have done that one!

I decided to have my boobs photographed professionally. I was beyond lucky enough to connect with an incredible photographer named Kristen Jensen, who photographed me for fucking free! I didn't know this at the time, but she started a huge fundraiser to help women such as myself and often photographed breast cancer patients and survivors at very little to no cost.

This beautiful woman is a model, an actress, a mother to a wonderful young man, a photographer that puts most others to shame, one who captures the true essence of a human being in her photos and a fiancé to a very lucky man. She is even more beautiful inside than she is out, and she's fucking gorgeous. Remember, I told you she's a fucking model!

Approximately four plus years after my first photo shoot in May of 2015, just prior to my double mastectomy, I asked this amazing woman if she could resend the photos she took back then. We had been in touch over the years but I waited to create a few prints from that photoshoot. Why, you ask? Why wait? I have a few reasons. First, I knew I was going to pay her for the prints and I had no fucking money. She was already so generous and I would never take advantage of anyone's generosity. Second, I didn't think I could bear to look at the breasts I lost. I wasn't ready. I was still "under construction" and wasn't sure I could bear to look at the beautiful breasts I no longer had. Third, the clock just kept ticking, life happened and time ran away from me.

So, this beautiful hearted soul sent me the pictures again and she didn't charge me a cent. Talk about generous! O.M.G. I never realized how beautiful they were! I showed my boyfriend the pictures, and he was absolutely amazed and speechless. He felt she truly captured ME and my true essence. It wasn't just about the boobs, given there were some pictures in which you couldn't really see all of them. He sincerely said, "I can see your picture on the front cover of a magazine." Holy fucking wowsers. Now, I can fully appreciate the old saying, "love is blind," but he is the type that says exactly what's on his mind and doesn't mince his words. His comments, unbeknownst to him, were repeated by my breastie when she saw the very same one he chose as his favorite.

I felt so ugly, so sad, so beaten up at the time. I couldn't see what they saw and quite obviously, what the photographer saw in me. I finally see it now given I'm in a much better place psychologically.

At one point during our conversation, this amazing photographer asked me to be one of her "courageous faces", one of her "models", in her 2019 upcoming breast cancer fundraiser. Holy fucking shit! Me? A model? I asked her some questions regarding her fundraiser and after sharing the details, she said, "You are one of the prettiest". I'm not sure she could ever realize how much that compliment meant to me, coming from someone so beautiful both inside and out.

I have often heard, "I wish you could see yourself through my eyes, the way I see you". Breast cancer is fucking ugly and it's scarring, internally and externally. It drains you of your self-esteem. It beats you up. It fucking hurts. But, the photographer's compliment, my boyfriend's incredible reaction to my pictures and my breastie's comments dove straight into my heart.

I graciously and excitedly agreed to participate in my photographer's October 2019 fundraiser, have my hair and make-up professionally done for free by a top notch participating salon and have an absolutely incredible new boob photo shoot. This phenomenal opportunity gifted me the opportunity to continue to share my story. After all, sharing is caring!!

I chose to photograph my boobs to get before and after pictures. This is how I dealt with losing them to that evil fucking disease, how I decided to memorialize them. These photos will be hanging up in my bedroom as a reminder of my fucking SURVIVAL!

Is memorializing your boobs important to you? Only you can answer that. You must do what's right for you at the time. And you know what? Any fucking thing you decide is right!

All photos taken by the beautiful Kristen Jensen.

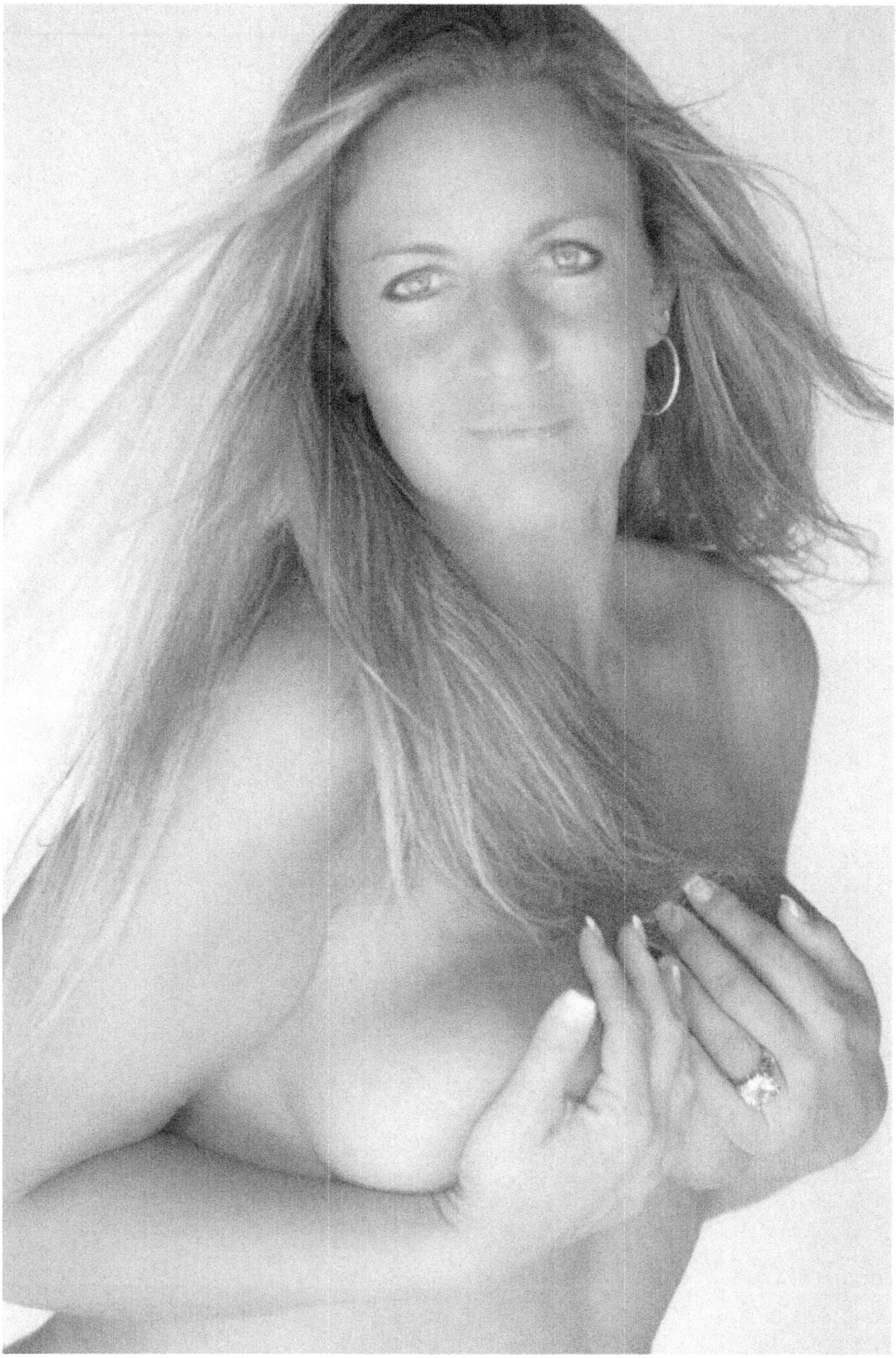

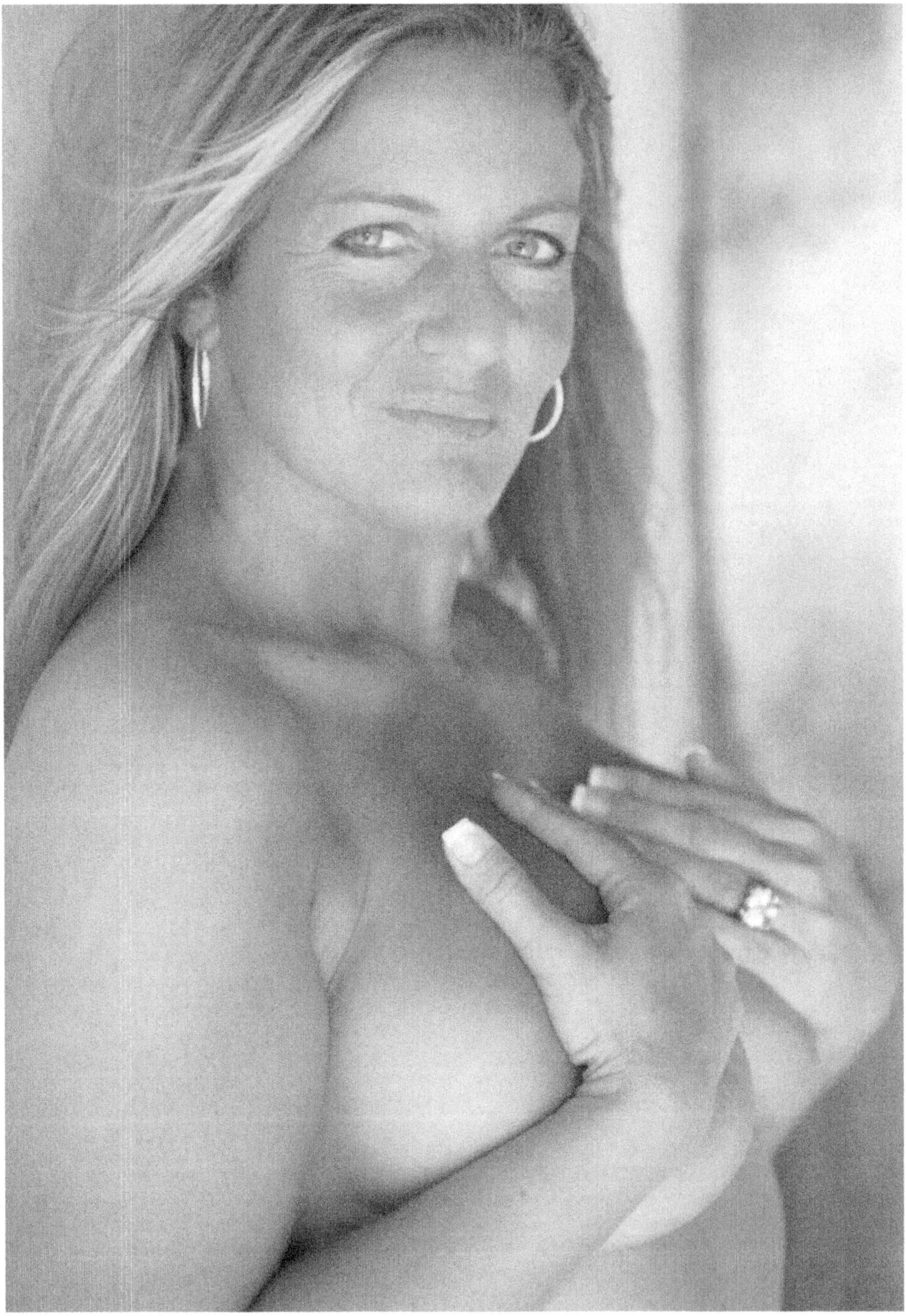

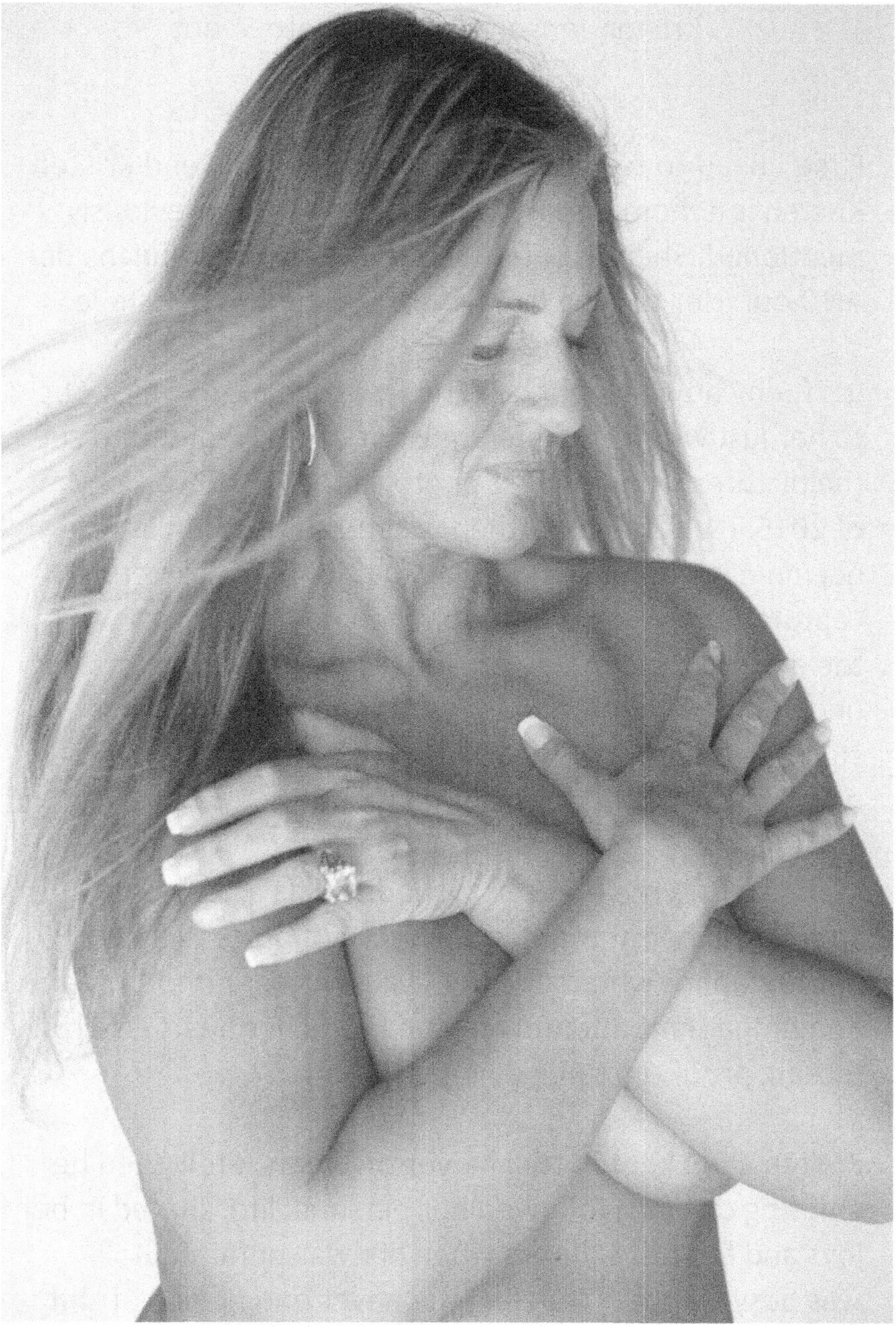

Chapter Fucking 30
Kristen Jensen and Our Photo Shoot

First, I need to tell you a little bit about my friend Kristen. Kristen is a mom, model and an actress, as I previously mentioned. She is utterly breathtakingly beautiful inside AND out. Her fucking heart is as beautiful as her smile.

It's funny how life works. Fate. I was meant to reach out to her just when I did. In August of 2019, I wanted to see the pictures from my first photo shoot which was in May of 2015. I was sad back then, scared shitless and at the beginning of an unknown scary ass journey. Kristen captured those moments from behind her camera with the eye of an incredible artist. She captured the uncertainties in me, the fears and the emotional shit storm that was brewing inside my head. That day in May of 2015 was the first time I met Kristen.

Kristen gifted me that photoshoot. I was a complete stranger to her at that time. She was a professional photographer who made her living with her photography. Remember I mentioned how beautiful her heart is? This is fucking proof right here.

Kristen and I kept in touch over the years. I followed her amazing career. I followed her personal life, shared in her joys and felt her sadness when life was unfair. But, life was busy for me, shoveling the never ending pile of shit that kept miraculously growing in my life.

January of 2019 was the start of good things in my life. All of a sudden, my karma changed. Good things started happening to me. New amazing job, new man, a little more money to pay off some debt, the tattoos on my breasts were done, my breasts were fucking done (at least for now!), my beautiful dog with cancer (osteosarcoma) was feeling better after thousands of dollars of treatments and amputation, my car was paid off, kids were both happy and doing well and the stars were finally fucking aligned! That fucking noose around my neck was gone. I could breathe again. I was making amends with my parents and my brother although nothing could ever be the same with them. I accepted that what happened fucking happened, sadly and disappointingly, but I learned. I learned that I shouldn't expect of others what I would expect of myself. I learned so much but that's another chapter in itself.

Kristen was so happy I reached out to her about my pictures from May of 2015. I never knew that she was such an active supporter of those with breast cancer. She founded an annual fundraising event called "Drink Pink" and 2019 would be her 11th year doing this. She asked me if I would consider being one of her models. YES!!! No fucking hesitation there!!!!!

I mentioned in my previous chapter how wonderful my day of beauty was at the top notch salon. That was preparation for the utterly incredible photo shoot I had with Kristen and her beautiful Mom. Kristen told me she could use a photo from four plus years ago but my energy is different now. Survivor fucking energy. She wanted to capture that in film, along with some of the tattoo work.

I went shopping and bought a ton of clothes to bring. I dug through my wardrobe and added more to the pile. Then, I went to find a bag for my shoes and realized I had a bag full of things from my very first trip with my boyfriend. Inside was a hot leather top I had brought to seduce him with. It worked, by the way – what a fucking awesome night that was!! I pulled it out of the bag, tried it on again and thought to myself, this would make a pretty hot picture. So, I stuck it in with all of the other clothes I was to bring for the photoshoot.

I arrived at Kristen's a bit early (so unlike me!). Her Mom was waiting for me and helped me set up all my things. Kristen arrived just a few minutes later and after hugs and kisses, we started going through all my clothes. She pulled out the leather top and said, "This is it!" Great minds, baby!!!

We started the photoshoot with the black leather top. She wanted fierce. Survivor mentality. Don't fuck with me attitude. She guided me through the session, encouraged me and brought out the fucking best in me. Kristen took amazing topless shots of me as well as some fully dressed. In fact, the pictures on the cover of this book are her work from that photoshoot!

Kristen chose twelve models for 2019's event. How incredibly lucky was I to be asked to be one of her twelve?! What a fucking honor! I have always wanted to share my story in the hopes of helping others. What a beautiful way to do so.

Last year, 2018, Kristen raised $27,000 and the money was donated to "Ann's Place", a community based cancer support organization. Organizations such as this one helped me during my darkest times. Support comes in so many ways – financial, emotional, physical, etc.

Kristen Jensen.

One woman who makes such a fucking impact in the lives of so many others.

One woman who made such a fucking impact on my life.

Kristen has been with me from the very beginning to the end of my breast cancer journey. From behind her camera, she captured the beginning of it and she captured the end of it. She is helping me help others by including me in such an awesome event and I couldn't be more honored.

Kristen empowered me in a way she will never understand.

Kristen gifted me a beautiful sense of closure.

I will forever be grateful.

Kristen Jensen and I during our second photo shoot, having a wonderful time!

Photo Credits for the portraits below go to the fabulous Kristen Jensen.

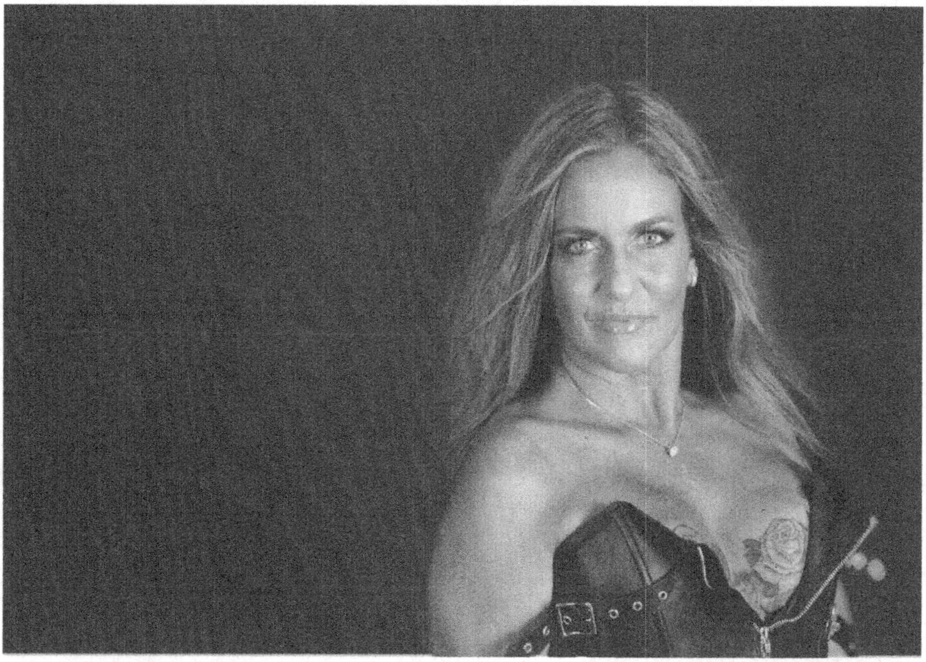

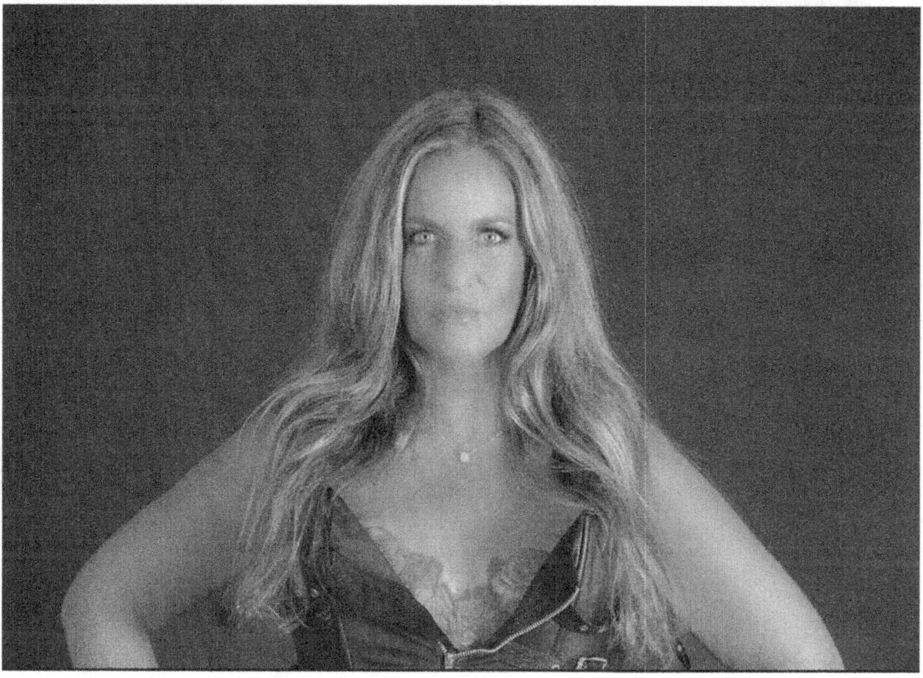

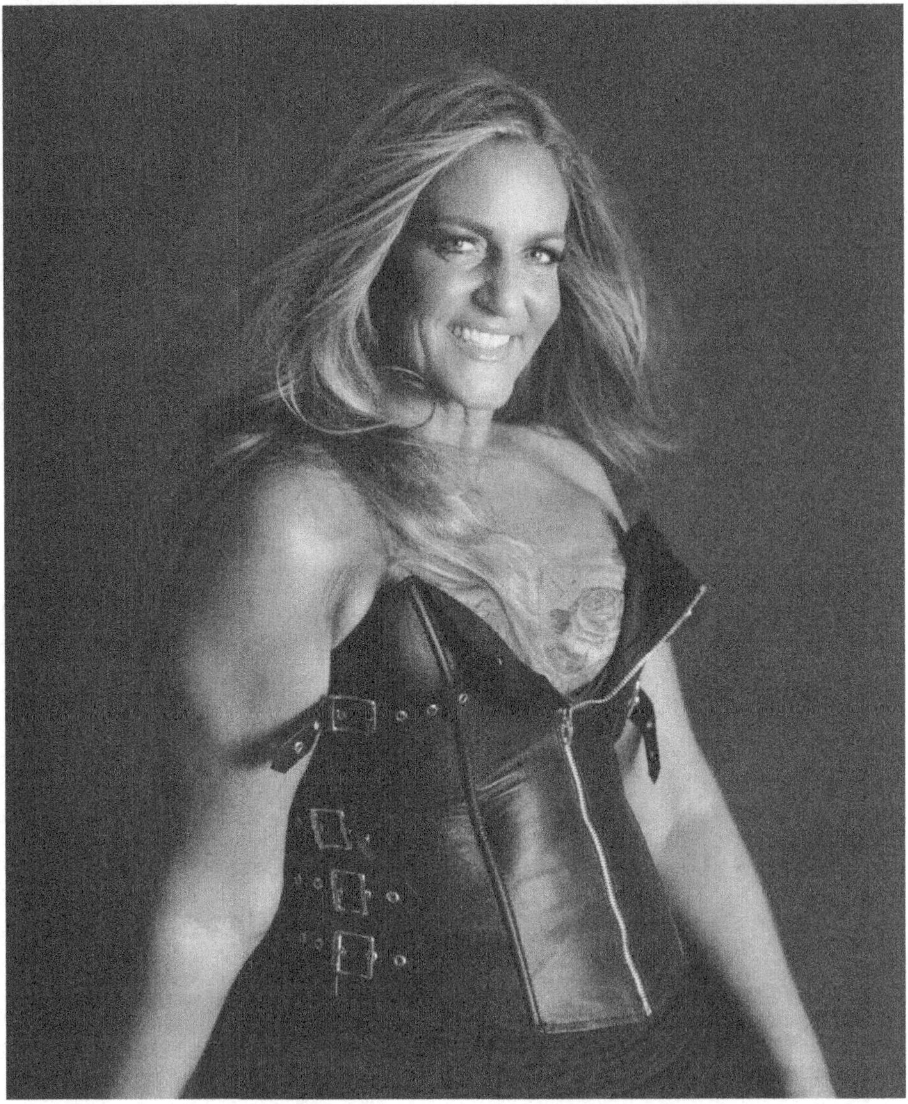

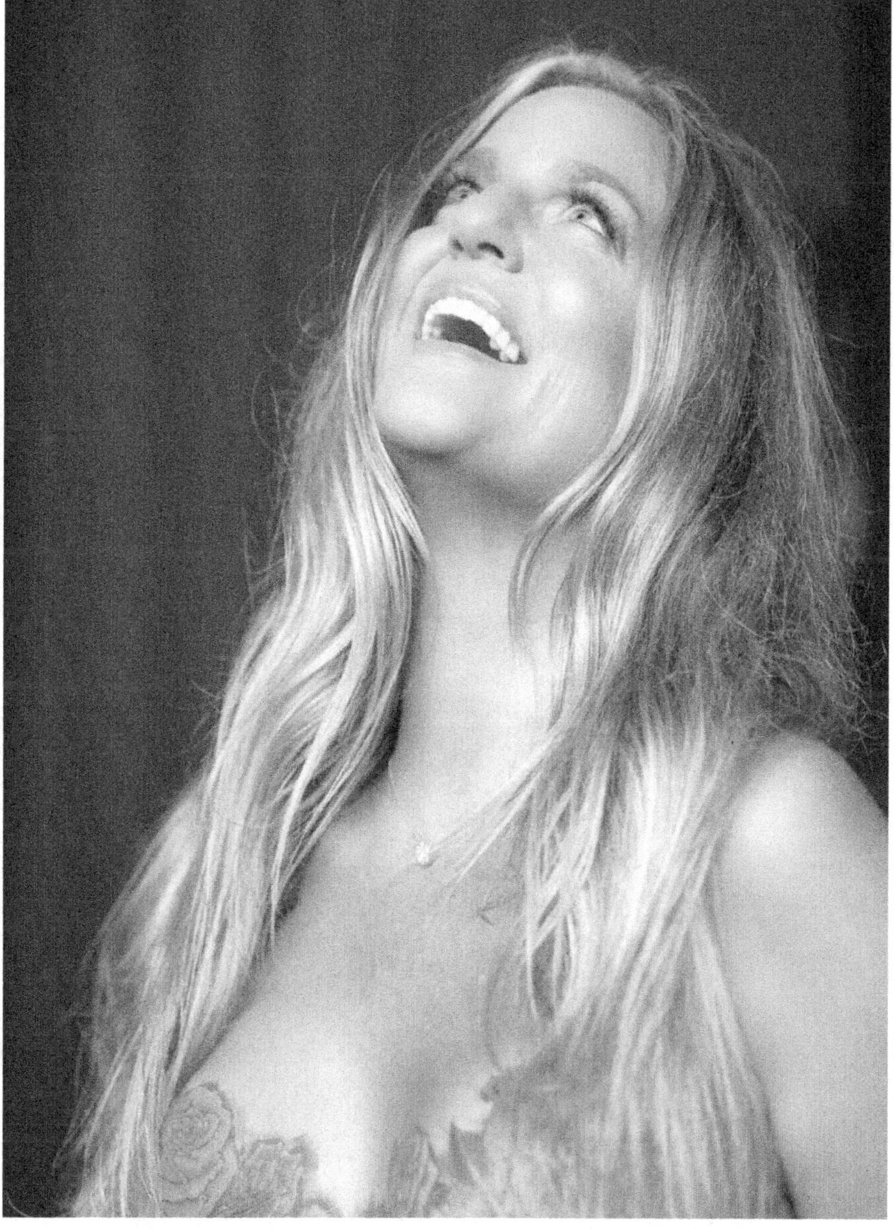

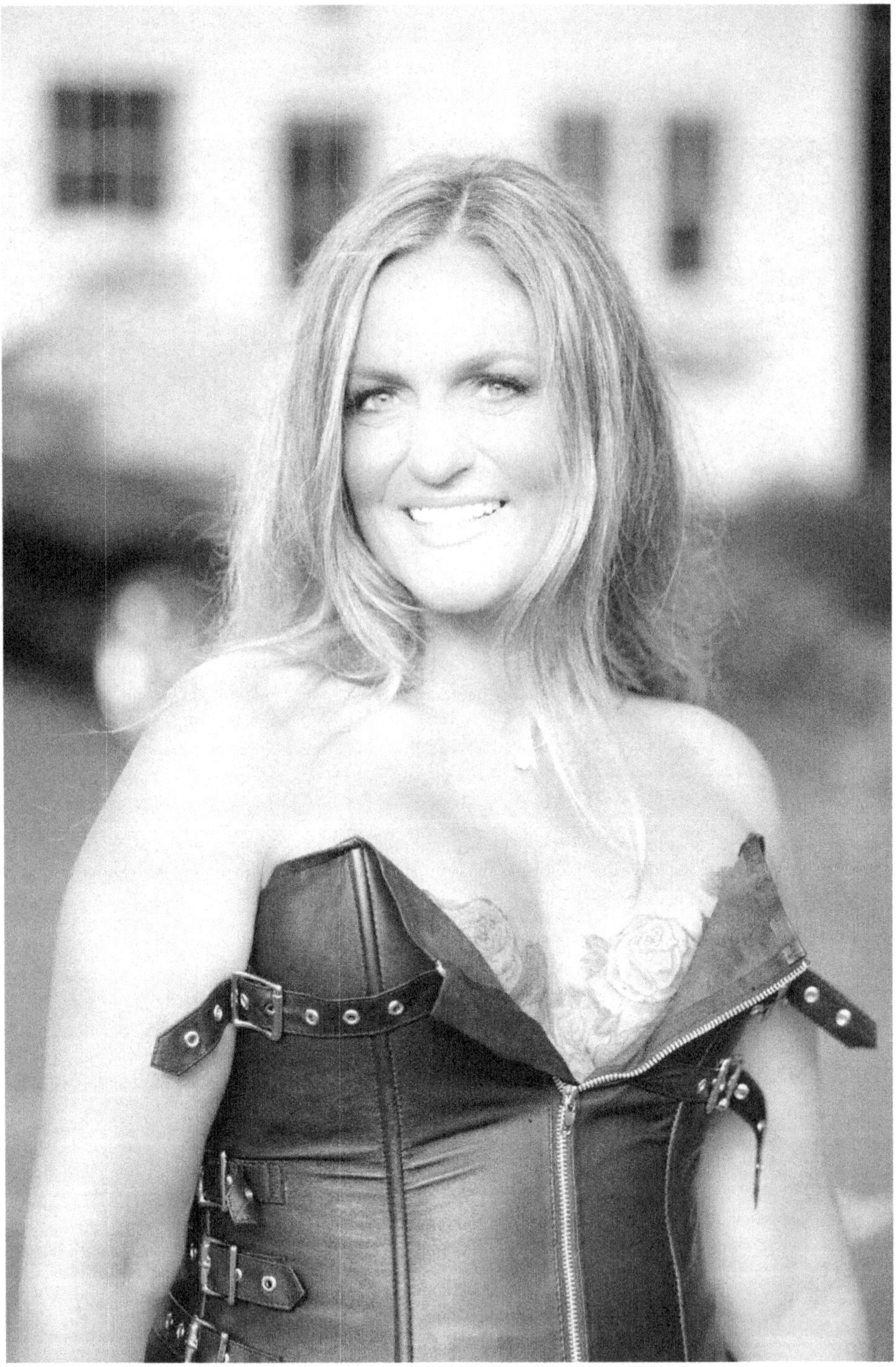

Chapter Fucking 31
Gummy Bear Projectile Missile Boob Recall

How fucking ironic is it that I receive a letter in the mail, four years post bitchy butcher surgery, stating that the textured implants I had were recalled?! The implants my bitchy butcher plastic surgeon decided to use have been linked to an increased incidence of BIA-ALCL. What the fuck is BIA-ALCL you ask?

It's FUCKING CANCER!!!

BIA-ALCL stands for "breast implant-associated anaplastic large cell lymphoma".

Yes, that's fucking cancer.

How ironic is it that all the shit I went through probably saved my life? It's times like these where it hits home. And hard. It makes you realize many things and although shit happens and it sucks, sometimes that shit prevents worse shit from happening. The old saying, "Everything happens for a reason" is just a way to make us feel better about bad shit in our lives. But in this case, I can honestly say I'm now grateful for that bitchy butcher fucking me up because I could be dead right now from BIA-ALCL!!

I didn't want the implants she chose. I didn't want these cancer causing projectile textured gummy bear implants. She did. Thank god I had issues starting that very day they were placed inside me. Thank god she fucked me up given she used those recalled implants and she was a butcher. Thank god I had serious infection and fever the very minute she placed those killers inside me. Thank god I had to find another plastic surgeon to clean up her mess. Thank god that amazing plastic surgeon had to remove those toxic implants. Thank god I had to have SIX more fucking painful breast surgeries to repair all the damage she caused. Thank god I went through hell and back all these years.

Thank god.

I am FUCKING ALIVE!

Things happen for a reason, don't they?! The bitchy butcher's fuck-ups resulted in my ultimate survival. My breast reconstruction took a serious hit but in the end, what matters is that I'm still here.

Trust the process, no matter what happens in life. Things suck along the way but ultimately, everything works out as it should. It's a hard lesson, each and every time, but know that the clock keeps ticking, life keeps happening, the sun keeps rising, we all keep getting older and tomorrow always comes whether we are here or not to experience it.

Know this…you are here today, right at this very moment, alive and breathing, reading my fucking book. Make the most of your "now", of your "today" because tomorrow

WILL come and who knows if we will be here for it. Keep turning these pages, laugh, cry, hug those you love, drink a big cup of coffee, smoke a little weed if it makes you feel better, run naked in the rain, make wild and passionate love, take that vacation, buy that dress you've been wanting, get your hair done, slow down a bit and take time for yourself.

Facing cancer in the fucking face and winning the battle creates a new sense of living for most of us. It has for me. It caused me to love every smell when I hopped on my motorcycle – freshly cut lawns, flowers and even manure never smelled so fabulous! The wind in my face made me feel so alive. Every sight, sound and smell should be appreciated because you are here TODAY. Enjoy TODAY. Live every minute of your life as fully as you can.

Stress is a killer as we all know yet who lives without it? Advice for you – try to minimize it. As I mentioned, shit happens all the time. It's how we deal with it that can increase or decrease our stress levels. I'd rather smile, laugh and love than fret, worry and get angry. Things always have a way of working out, one way or another. And as you read just a couple of minutes ago, there may be reasons for the way shit unfolds that you won't understand until that moment, years later. That "AHA" moment, that realization that things happened for a fucking reason!

So the next time something shitty happens or you get shitty news, take a moment to reflect on what that crazy foul mouthed author just told you. Life keeps happening and things will get better. What's the fucking lesson to be learned here? Don't let anything get you down and if it does, don't let it get you down for long. Remember those fucking pots of gold at the end of the rainbow? Yours is waiting for you.

Chapter Fucking 32
Pink Fucking Crown In My Mouth

What the fuck does a visit to the dentist have to do with breast cancer? Well I'm going to fucking tell you! Sit your ass down and listen up.

I was told I needed a crown. Somehow, this crazy brain of mine impulsively sent a message to my mouth and out came, "I'd like a pink one!" A pink one, they said. They had never seen a pink crown before. I said, "Yes, I had breast cancer and I'd love a pink crown." Despite finding me a bit odd and quirky, which I am, they loved the idea!

I was given a temporary crown while my pink crown was being made. A few weeks later, I was called in to have the pink crown "installed". Well, this pink crown came out pretty nasty looking. There was no fucking way I was putting that dirty looking thing in my mouth full of pearly whites! Pink would work. Not a fuddy duddy dirty tooth. I was so excited to see my pink crown – get it? Pink crown for this pink breast cancer survivor princess. Talk about a huge disappointment. I looked at this tiny little specimen of a crown in disgust. The dentist looked at this tiny little specimen of a crown in disgust as well. I looked at her and asked, "Would you put that in your mouth?" Her response, "Absolutely not!"

They re-ordered the crown. I waited a few more weeks, bought a bunch of Poly-grip given my temporary kept falling out and finally was called back in. The crown came back but this time, it was white. What the fuck?! I waited all this time for a white crown? No fucking way! Send that shit back!

They were apologetic given the lab messed up again. Thankfully, I loved this office and everyone in it. They called me a few days later, letting me know that they couldn't do pink but they could paint a pink ribbon on the front of the white crown.

PERFECTION.

My little crown, sitting on the last tooth in the right lower side of my mouth, has a pink breast cancer ribbon on it. Now how fucking cool is that?! My crown and I became quite famous in that office. Cell phones came out of everyone's pockets, pictures of my crown were taken from all different angles, my crown was posted all over Facebook and other social media outlets and I became their first client to have such a creative breast cancer survivor crown.

Nothing but the best for this breast cancer Warrior Princess!!!

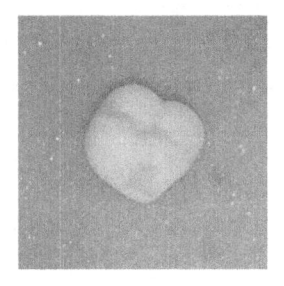

Chapter Fucking 33
My Fucking Breast Tattoos

I'm going to tell you a fucking wild story. It dates back to May of 2015. I was just diagnosed with the awful "C" word and was sitting on my deck, tanning topless, in preparation for my boob photo shoot. I had decided I wanted a tattoo, my "survival stamp". So, I grabbed around four or five yellow pieces of paper. Why yellow, you wonder? I don't fucking know!

I sat outside, on my deck in a lounge chair, with a small table next to me. I started to draw out the design I was envisioning in my head. The problem is that I can't fucking draw anything other than bubble letters and stick figures. I went through each and every piece of paper, scribbling out each and every attempt until finally, I drew something that I loved. I excitedly yelled out, "That's it!".

Happily, I piled all the pieces of paper onto the table and leaned back into my lounge chair with a huge smile of accomplishment. I was absolutely thrilled I finally came up with a design I loved.

It was a perfect spring day – beautiful dry weather, no wind, comfortable temperature, just fucking perfect. All of a sudden, a huge gust of wind comes out of fucking nowhere. It picks up my stack of yellow papers, throws them up in the air and over the side of the deck. What the fuck?! "Noooooooo!!!!!" I jump up to try and salvage a few pieces but no such luck. I cover my breasts as I do so because of course, I have neighbors and want to be somewhat appropriate. (Side note, can you imagine me wanting to be appropriate? I'm cracking up! But yes, even with this mouth and view on fucking cancer, I'm a class act of a lady - insert chuckle here!!) With a feeling of dread, I looked over the top of the railing and saw all my hard work blow into the pricker bushes. Now, I live in the fucking woods. There are wild animals and ticks and gross things out there not to mention all the dangerous wild blackberry bushes.

My heart sunk. I sat back down in my lounge chair, leaned back, let out a huge sigh of disappointment and closed my eyes. A minute or so later, I opened my eyes, turned my head and happened to look at the little table next to me. Wait a hot fucking minute here. Did I see one yellow page still sitting on that table? Holy shit I did! I leaned forward, not expecting anything much given "the chosen one" was on the top of the pile and was probably long gone.

I picked up the lonely yellow piece of paper and you'll never guess what the fuck happened. It was the one! The top piece of paper was still fucking there!! Now, how does that happen?! That gust of wind, the ONLY gust of wind that whole fucking day, picks up all of the yellow pieces of paper, blows all of them into the air and over the deck EXCEPT the TOP piece with my chosen tattoo drawn on it. I was in amazement and said to myself, "This is a sign!"

I've learned that there are signs, tons of signs out there. Do you notice them? Pay the fuck attention, people. Signs are messages but we need to be willing to acknowledge and listen to them. Open your eyes and you'll see them too.

So, needless to say, I got that tattoo as soon as I was able to. I have horrible handwriting – one job even told me such in a three month review given that's all they could find wrong with me. Now that made me laugh and still does, but I knew I didn't want my messy writing forever inked on my body. I asked my beautiful daughter to clean it up for me. She did. At the age of twelve, her handwriting was far superior to mine. Her writing is now forever preserved on my body. How fucking special is that?!

This beautiful tattoo was placed on my right side, over my rib cage. It fucking hurt. I didn't know of any tattoo artists so I impulsively walked into a place without an appointment. Unfortunately, the tattoo artist I got was new and didn't place it the way I wanted so one of the words actually looks like it is upside the fuck down. When he was done torturing me (this little tattoo took hours despite not needing to take that fucking long and cost far too much), I excitedly looked in the mirror, and thought the mirror was playing tricks on me. What the fuck? I said, "I think there's a mistake. One of the words is upside down." He defensively said to me, "That's what you wanted!" I said, so very nicely, "I didn't want anything upside down." I think that's fair to say. The problem was that he angled the tattoo given he thought it would look better placed alongside the contours of my ribs and in doing so, one of the words turned upside down.

But, you know the fuck what? I LOVE my upside down tattoo!!! And you know what else? IT IS WHAT IT FUCKING IS!!!!!!

Initially, I figured I'd travel to Virginia to have my nipples and areolas tattooed by an expert. This tattoo artist specializes in three dimensional nipple and areola tattoos. I wasn't going to chance another fuck up, not with my boobs!!! Unfortunately, my fucking tits looked horrendous once the bitchy butcher was done slaughtering them but something had to be done.

After all my surgeries, I decided there was no fucking way I could put nipples and areolas on these puppies. I started exploring other options and came up with full breast tattoo coverage. ME. Covering my breasts in fucking tattoos. I fucking loved the idea!!! I searched for ideas on line for the fuck ever it seemed. I finally found a design I loved - a bouquet of roses splayed all across my breasts. Feminine. Beautiful.

I wanted to look in the mirror and fucking smile. I cried every day when I saw them looking all puckered, dimpled and deformed. I didn't just see fucked up breasts. That's not what brought the tears. I looked in the mirror and saw "loss". My breasts pre-tattoo work were a constant reminder of all I lost from this fucking disease – I lost my breasts, my family, my business, my son for a short time, money, tons of fucking money, my happy life as I thought I knew it. These tears occurred every fucking day. I knew I had to do it. I had to disguise the disfigurement so that I could move on with my life.

I was in amazement when I saw before and after pictures of other women who went this route. I met a tattoo artist through the biker world who offered to tattoo my breasts for fucking FREE once I was done with all of my surgeries. I couldn't believe the kind offer. In fact, another tattoo artist offered the same. People DO have hearts! Money was non-existent and tattoos aren't cheap.

May 21st, 2018, I started my breast tattoos with this tattoo artist. He squeezed me in between customers. This was the first time in his 30 plus years of tattooing that he tattooed a breast cancers survivor's breasts. He used organic ink and went slow. By the end of 2018, the work was almost complete. He decided to close his shop so I went to another wonderful tattoo artist to fill in a couple of little areas that wasn't able to be completed. You can see some of the tattoos on the cover of this book. They are absolutely gorgeous! I can't even begin to describe how much of an impact the breast tattoos have made on my life, on my self-confidence and on my healing process. Many women don't even know this option exists and they should!

I don't fucking cry anymore when I look in the mirror.

I smile.

In fact, I LOVE looking at my breasts now. I fucking LOVE when they peek out of my tops. It's my fucking MASTERPIECE. I worked fucking HARD for these. I worked fucking HARD to succeed. To live. I want other women to know that this is a beautiful option to consider.

I have a picture here that shows the upper parts of my tattoos. If you are a breast cancer survivor and are interested in seeing what they look like in their entirety, please contact me. I'm happy to meet with you and show you so that you can see for yourselves. Both of my wonderful breast surgeons fell in love with them – Dr. Beth Sieling, my breast surgeon that removed my breasts and Dr. Mark, the wonderful plastic surgeon that fixed them after they were butchered by the first bitchy butcher of a plastic surgeon.

It cracks me up when I wear something that shows part of my ink. I dress very girly girl. Always have and always will. In fact, I used to ride my Harley with a dress on! I can't even begin to tell you how many stares and double takes people make because this refined girly girl has a little ink! I've always loved a little shock factor.

I now have closure. My breast cancer journey is fucking over. My breasts are now beautiful again, four long fucking years later. I can smile. I can move forward. I can love myself again.

I feel whole.

This tattoo that was gifted to me is something I will forever be grateful for.

Tattoos aren't just for biker chicks anymore!

Chapter Fucking 34
Drink Pink Event 2019

What an incredible honor it was, to be asked by Kristen Jensen to participate in this breast cancer fundraiser. I mention it in a previous chapter, but here is a little more detail on the event. I'm writing this prior to the actual event so at this point I can't comment on how fabulous I KNOW it will be, how liberating it will be to share my story, how fulfilling to be a part of such a wonderful cause, how strong I know I will feel, how confident and beautiful I will feel that night all dressed up, make-up and hair done, how proud I will feel with the man of my dreams by my side and knowing how proud he is of me, how loved and supported I will feel by all those in my life who are able to come out and support me and my cause.

Sometimes I think I'm dreaming. My life has come full circle. It brings tears to my fucking eyes. If this hasn't yet happened to you, it will. Keep the faith, bitch. It'll fucking happen. Take advice from this bitch who fucking went through it. And I say "bitch" lovingly, just to add emphasis. We can all be bitchy of course, but you're no bitch. Well, maybe you are. What the fuck do I know! Listen, stop being a bitch and smile, embrace life and turn that fucking frown upside down.

Back to the wonderful event……

All of the women featured shared their stories in a news publication. In fact, a woman named Kerry Anne so generously volunteered her time to publish a write-up of each and every Courageous Face model. Each girl's picture and their responses to Kerry Anne's questions are included. Here is mine. I had to keep it clean given it was going out to the general public, but just know I wanted to add the word "fuck" a whole shitload of times! It's not just because I fucking love the word "fuck", but because there's no other way, in my twisted and demented mind, to fully express how I feel without the huge emphasis the word "fuck" adds when used.

QUESTION: In prep for your photoshoot with Kristen Jensen, you got your beauty on at Adam Broderick salon & spa! Tell me about your photo shoot with Kristen and beauty day at Adam Broderick.

ME: I felt like a princess!! I went for my hair and make-up at Adam Broderick's salon and was treated like royalty. What an amazing feeling after four long years of surgeries, pain and tears. I then went for the most amazing photo shoot with the most amazing woman and photographer of all times. Kristen has a natural way of bringing out the absolute best in you, she has a way of making you feel comfortable and beautiful and she makes the photo shoot such fun!! She is as beautiful inside as she is out and I'm truly blessed to know her. I am so thankful for this amazing experience and will forever remember my special day.

QUESTION: When and how did you first learn you had breast cancer?

ME: I had issues with my left breast for close to a year and was closely monitored. Unfortunately, all the tests continued to come back as "inconclusive". Approximately one year after I noticed the original issue, on May 15, 2015, I was finally diagnosed with breast cancer. I had Ductal Carcinoma in Situ with Invasive Ductal Carcinoma. On May 27, 2015, I had a double mastectomy. Eight major breast surgeries later, I am cancer free and loving life!

QUESTION: Who did you turn to for support and how was that person or organization supportive?

ME: Thankfully, I had the love and support of my two beautiful children and a couple of close friends. I was directed to a social worker at a cancer center and she assisted in helping me acquire some financial assistance given I was a single mother and unable to work. These organizations that help women such as myself are a godsend for those of us who need assistance. It's extremely difficult and humiliating to ask for help, but when you are sick and responsible for two young children, you truly have no choice. I will forever be grateful for the support and assistance I received.

QUESTION: Tell me about something someone said or did that helped you through your most difficult days

ME: My daughter was my biggest supporter. She was 12 years old when I was diagnosed. She immediately painted the pink ribbon on one of her nails as soon as she learned about my diagnosis. She wrote inspirational messages on post its and placed them all over my desk. She always told me, "You are more than your breasts!" She helped me through every surgery. She saw my breasts take and lose shape over and over and continued to love and support me. She always thought I was beautiful no matter what I looked like. She came to breast cancer fundraisers with me. She was a constant in my life when nothing else was and continues to be my very best friend.

QUESTION: What message do you have for others who have been diagnosed with breast cancer?

ME: I am authoring a book on breast cancer which will give some wonderful yet bluntly stated insight and advice (it will be out soon), but in the meantime, here is my advice…breast cancer sucks. There is no eloquent way to say it. My heart aches for all those going through what I went through but just know, although the journey is downright awful, it will bring you to a new and wonderful destination. I went through eight major breast surgeries – two that botched me and six more that fixed the mess. Thankfully, the last six of the eight surgeries were by an amazing surgeon who made me feel whole again. You, too, will feel whole. You will heal. Cry when you need to cry. Ask for help when you need the help. And know you're not alone in anything you are feeling. Whatever you decide is best for you, is. Trust yourself, love yourself and fully live every minute of your life. Keeping a positive attitude, despite the tears, is so important. You will get through this!!!

Chapter Fucking 35
I Have A Fucking Voice and I'm Gonna Fucking Use It

Can you believe this chick was quiet and shy growing up? Fuck yea! I had to be pushed into a room. I never spoke out loud. I was a good student, a kind person, I went with the flow, I wore dresses every day until I was five (I still wear dresses every day!), I had good grades all my life except in college, I always said "yes" even when I should have said "no", I gave and gave and still give and give selflessly, I never disagreed with anyone, I never spoke the fuck up.

I just went with the fucking flow.

Here's a fucking example for you. Trombones. Why the fuck am I mentioning trombones? You'll see why in a second or two…just keep reading.

It was fifth grade and time to select an instrument. Here I go again, going with the fucking flow. Did I need to be in the band? Did I want to be in the band? Not really. My father encouraged music given he played the trombone and mastered in music.

When presented with choices, I was given three. Trombone #1, trombone #2 or trombone #3. Hmmmmmm……tough choice. My father had three trombones. The choice was already made. I had to play the trombone. I, of course, acquired the rusted old ugly embarrassing trombone to start with and it was bigger than me when I started. I eventually worked my way up to trombone #2 which I still have and truly love given it was a part of my life for twelve years.

I went with the fucking flow.

I played that fucker all the way through college. I performed. I competed. I blew and blew and blew. I can joke about my blowing here but that might be fucking inappropriate.

Guess the fuck what? Surprise, surprise...I no longer go with the fucking flow. Fuck that! Life is too fucking short to waste time not being true to myself. I found my voice. I found my strength. I learned I can only count on myself when the chips are down. I had always let people take advantage of my kindness. I'm still guilty of that given it's hard to change innately who you are. I feel good giving to others, helping others, protecting others, nurturing others, seeing others happy. In fact, and how fucking miserable is this thought, I always felt it was ok for others to find their happiness but it was ok if I didn't.

Now that's fucked up. And, finally, I can say that fucked up view has changed. I deserve happiness just like the next person does.

This makes me think of my upbringing. Of course, isn't that what therapists do? I thought I was loved. I felt loved. I believe my parents did what they thought was best in their minds. But I had no voice. I'm not quite sure if I wasn't allowed to use it, if I wasn't encouraged to use it or if I was forced not to.

This now brings me back to the breast cancer because ultimately, that's what this fucking book is about. When I was faced with the problems with my left breast, I went to all of my doctors myself. I went for all of my testing myself. I went for all biopsies myself. I even went for my fucking diagnosis myself. I sat in that office alone with my amazeballs breast surgeon Dr. Beth Sieling, and heard those words, "You have cancer". I cried alone. I chose the surgeons I was to use (of course, the bitchy butcher plastic surgeon was a referral and not a choice I'm proud of!). I chose the hospitals, given that's where my surgeons operated. I made my own fucking decisions and it seemed as if my family wasn't too happy about that. I used my own voice. I stood on my own two feet and took care of myself.

No more control of little Cindy. Cindy was a big girl making her own fucking decisions. Control. I truly believe I allowed myself to be controlled my whole fucking life.

Cancer rocked my world in so many ways. It knocked me down. It beat me up. It scarred me inside and out. It robbed me of so many things and ultimately, it changed the reality of my life.

What is really important in life? Is your life truly as you think it is or as you imagine it to be? Are you truly happy?

Do you use your fucking voice? Do you speak up for yourself?

People, listen to your gut. Make your own fucking decisions. If people stick around, they truly love you. If they don't because they can't control you, fuck 'em. My family didn't stick around. In fact, they fucking abandoned me at a time I needed them the most. Why? I will never understand it. The decisions I made were, in my mind, at the time, the best decisions I could make. A little fucking respect would have been nice.

Am I fucking hurt from this? You bet your ass I am. Have I been able to move forward? Absolutely. Life is too fucking short to wallow in self misery, pain and anger. Will I ever forget? No fucking way. Can I ever forget? Nope. That shit happened and will forever be in my head. Unfortunately. The type of relationship I thought I once had with my family was truly different than what I actually had.

But, with that said, I am moving forward. I still love my parents. I realize they are who they are. Are they bad people? No. Did they do something beyond incomprehensible, utterly disgusting and downright selfish? Yes. Can I forgive them? I'm not one who preaches the benefits of forgiving. I preach moving forward. Shit fucking happens. Through life, we experience and we learn. This is my family, whether I like what they did or not, and I still love them. I don't respect them for their actions but I can move forward. It took a few years and many tears to fully realize this. Progress can be slow but it can happen.

We learn from our experiences. We grow. We become stronger. Reality hurts but it forces you to move the fuck forward.

Whatever your decision is, it's yours. You own it. Don't let anyone control your destiny. Choices we make can be life or death so let it be your choice. Speak up for yourself.

Don't play the fucking trombone if you want to play the flute.

I found my FUCKING VOICE.

FIND YOURS!!

Chapter Fucking 36
Fight Song by Rachel Platten

One day, as I was feeling so fucking sorry for myself, a song came on the radio that screamed to my soul.

"Fight Song" by Rachel Platten, is a song that brings tears to my eyes every time I hear it. I don't know Rachel but I'd like to publicly thank the shit out of her for releasing this song just when I needed to hear it the most.

There are songs you hear that are catchy but you really don't listen to the words. In fact, you have absolutely no fucking clue what the song is about but you sing along anyway.

Then there are songs you hear that stop you dead in your tracks, empower you, leave your jaw dropped open and have you thinking, "What the fuck! That song was meant for me!" I call those songs messages from the universe, words you need to hear just when you need to hear them. In other words, a fucking form of synchronicity.

I still hear that song on the radio and I still cry every single time. In fact, I'm fucking crying now as I write this, just thinking of the song. You all know what I'm talking about because you have all experienced this...music is a beautiful, poetic form of expression.

We all have our own battles to fight in this ferris wheel of life and it's helpful to grasp onto whatever can help you survive.

Rachel, I want you to know, I have taken my life back. I have fought back. I have won! And you know what? I agree with the lyrics in your song – I don't give a fuck what anyone else thinks, I proved to myself that I'm a strong mother fucker and I am fucking ALIVE to write this book. Thank you for this incredibly empowering song that carried me through my darkest times. It will always be one of my favorites.

Chapter Fucking 37
My Family Re-cap

Life happens.

I think that's the best fucking way to explain why things happen the way they do.

My family, as I once knew it, is gone. Changed. Forever. I am done mourning the loss of what I always thought it was and now accept the reality of what it is and what it quite possibly always was. I just never allowed myself to see that reality either as a form of self-protection or I was just in plain ol' denial.

Reality struck so fucking hard. It was hard enough to deal with all the shit I've dealt with in my life, never mind adding breast cancer to the mix. It made it that much harder to deal knowing I lost my family when I needed them the most. But, in the end, I learned how to fucking survive. I am so much stronger than I ever was.

My life took on a whole new fucking direction and I absolutely LOVE it.

In fact, I LOVE who I am.

And you know the fuck what? I still love my family...well, most of them. I love my parents and accept who and what they are. I love my brother and accept who and what he is. They aren't the same people I thought I knew all those years but I accept them as I now know them.

My parents and my brother are now in my life in one form or another. I still tell them, "I love you", because I do. I wish only happiness for all of them. I realize my parents had their own issues given they got divorced soon after my breast cancer diagnosis. In fact, I can't believe they waited that long to get divorced given they were miserable a good portion of their marriage.

Life goes on, it fucking evolves and you have no choice but to hang on tight for the ride. One day, that fucking ride will stop, thank god. You'll find your footing again and despite not being able to make sense of everything, you'll find your new norm. I found my new norm with my family. Is it as wonderful as I once thought it to be? No fucking way. Can I trust my family the way I thought I once could? No. Can I rely on them as I thought I could before June 2nd,2015, when they walked out of my life? No. I consider all of this part of life's lessons.

I found my way, on my own. You can do it, too. If you have the love and support of those around you, you're in a much better place but know you can do it just as I did. Family doesn't need to be blood related, it is chosen so choose wisely.

I fucking overcame everything thrown my way and I'll continue to do so. I don't try to make it sound easy because it was one of the hardest things I've ever been through, one of the most painful. I often say, the pain of losing my family at a time I needed them the most hurt more than the pain and fears of having breast cancer and eight major breast surgeries. I suffered a shit load of loss, all hitting me at the same time, but IT IS WHAT IT FUCKING IS.

Remember my saying that got me through so much shit, because it can help you in your darkest moments….scream it out loud and laugh like a crazy mother fucker after you yell it…then just let it go…

IT IS WHAT IT FUCKING IS!

Chapter Fucking 38
Deb, My Bestie of 37 Plus Years

Deb and I have been friends since I was twelve years old. (Yep – I'm getting old!) Deb is the type of girl who says it like it is, adding a "fuck or two, or three" in her vocabulary for emphasis. I always know I can rely on her to tell me if my butt looks big, if my hair looks ok, if my eyebrows need waxing or if I need a fucking pedicure which I currently do…she WANTS the best for me and always has. Now, that's a REAL fucking friend.

Deb and I have joked for years that we will become our own version of The Golden Girls. We have gone through marriages together, divorces, kids, family issues, illness, even death. We laugh together, we cry together and we are always there for each other no matter what. Judgment free zone.

She is the sister I never had…well, by birth, I have a blood sister but a very selfish, self-absorbed one I haven't spoken to in many years, one who was not there in any way during my battle with breast cancer, nor my divorce, etc. In fact, many years ago, she once told me, "I've been a bad sister to you," which I wholeheartedly agreed to. Another time, when I had just confided in her that my soon to be ex-husband deleted our bank account at the beginning of my divorce, she snootily said, "I have so much money I don't know what to do with it all".

Back to Deb, my sister by choice...Deb was there for every surgery. Deb brought me to two out of three of the plastic surgeons I chose for a second opinion. Deb's family was mine and mine was hers. She couldn't believe all the shit my family put me through and she lost a ton of respect for them. She stuck by me through it all. She included me in all of her family celebrations, as she always did. She was, is and will always be my bestie and my sister.

Close to a week after my double mastectomy, Deb insisted she take Julia and I out to lunch. I had nothing to wear! Try fitting those fucking drains inside a dress and try not to make it look obvious. Well, after trying on at least five or six dresses, we figured it out. Don't forget, I couldn't lift my arms so that was quite an adventure! It was exhausting, the whole process, finding something to wear, making myself presentable and sitting at the table for so long. But, Deb knew, it was good for my fucking psyche. I needed to get out yet I didn't know it. Deb did. We had a lovely girls lunch out, the three of us. Don't forget my little Julia – she was my biggest supporter!!!

Deb always understood me and to this day, she will tell you that I did NOTHING to warrant my family's behavior. Deb witnessed EVERYTHING for herself given she was around so often and she knows my family so well.

One day, a couple of months after my double mastectomy, Deb says, "Let's go see this movie – it's about two women who grew up together, best friends, a blonde like you and a brunette like me." So, we go out for dinner and head over to the movie theater. The theater was pretty quiet but of course, these two bitchy women have to sit directly in front of us. Isn't that always how it goes?

Deb and I were quietly talking while the commercials were going. The previews hadn't even begun. The women in front of us turned around and "shushed" us. What the fucckkkk??!! Don't fucking "shush" me! Of course, we had a few words, a few loud words. These "women" were a bit rough around the edges and crass so all I could think of was, I'm getting some soda thrown in my face, a punch in the gut, maybe beat up in the parking lot after. Oh shit, my breast expanders may burst. Great. Just fucking great. Oh well. The movie began.

It's always fun being with Deb and the idea that this movie was about two lifelong friends appealed to us both. There was the blonde, me. There was the brunette, Deb. The blonde was diagnosed with breast cancer. Wait a hot fucking minute, what was this movie about?! I looked at Deb, my jaw dropped open, my eyes bulged. She turned her head to me at the very same time, with the same exact look on her face. She said, "I had no idea!" We, and very loudly I should add, bawled the entire movie. The ending was absofuckinglutely horrible. The blonde died. NOT what I fucking needed to see at that time in my life.

We left that movie hysterically crying. I sobbed, "I don't want to die! Deb, how could you bring me to see this movie?!" Amidst her tears, she said, "I really didn't know! I'm so so sorry! I don't want you to die either!"

We got to her car, and all of a sudden, we both started laughing, uncontrollably. Breast cancer patient almost gets beat up in a movie theater watching a movie about a woman with breast cancer. That would make for quite an interesting headline! We still laugh about that today. Only my Deb would bring me to this movie...but I must say, it was a fuckingly fabulously tear jerking movie. Just bad timing!

Deb is my soul sister, my confidante, she never judges me and loves and accepts me as I am. I am so blessed to have such an amazing woman in my life who loves me, supports me, laughs with me, believes in me and will always be there for me. My hope is that all of you have someone in your life like Deb.

I love you, Deb!!!

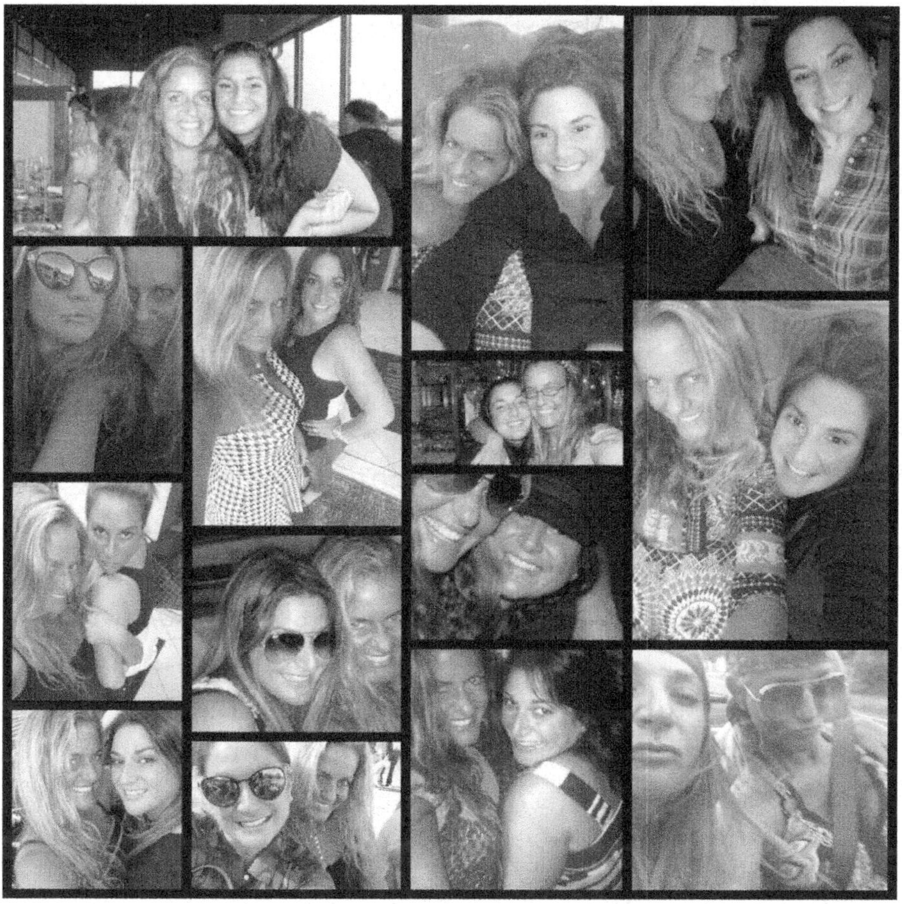

Chapter Fucking 39
Magical Night at Drink Pink

The worst day of my life began when I was diagnosed with cancer
Are you sure? Can't be, that happens to others
I've got two kids, four dogs, a mortgage to pay
A single Mom alone, for survival I pray

Twelve days of chaos from diagnosis to losing my breasts
Tears and fears consumed me, I was so depressed
I loved my breasts but they had to go
Who knew my life as I knew it would take such a blow

I met a beautiful photographer named Kristen
A woman full of kindness, sincerity and compassion
She offered to capture my breasts on film before I lost them
A gift for a stranger, a generosity I've not seen often

She captured the moment with perfection and grace
Sadness but strength written all over my face
The experience, the photos, her kindness and love
Started me on my journey, one I never dreamed of

Losing my breasts was hard enough
Lost my business, close family, life was so rough
Desperate for help, couldn't ask, too proud
Lost and confused, I'd get through this I vowed

My journey lasted four years, my worst years ever
So much loss, sadness, my life changed forever
The wicked paths I was forced to take
Scarred me inside and out, but I did not break

Four years later and I'm here and alive
Efffff you cancer, I efffffin' survived!
I'm breathing, I'm laughing, my life is in tact
This girl as you know it, watch out, she's back!

Kristen asked me to be one of her Courageous Faces
In Drink Pink, her breast cancer fundraiser for Ann's Place
What an honor to be asked, such a beautiful ending
To this journey I've travelled, or is it my beginning?

Generously treated to a day of beauty at Adam Broderick's Salon
Followed by a fabulous photo shoot by Kristen Jensen
This second shoot four years later captured my truth
Survival, strength, Kristen knew all I went through

Leather top, tattoos exposed, fierce look in my eyes
She encouraged the warrior from deep inside
I fought this and won, I'm thrilled to share
She nailed my thoughts through my stance and my glare

Dressed like Cinderella attending a ball
Pink dress, bling purse, shimmery shoes, hair, make up and all
What an amazing way to end this journey of hell
Or is it my new beginning, this story to tell

Looking out at the sea of faces, some with tears and most with smiles
Feeling overwhelmed with thoughts of love and survival
Tears slipped from my eyes, emotions I couldn't control
I made it, I beat it, I finally feel whole

The evening was a fairy tale, an experience so surreal
I woke the next morning, was it a dream or was it real?
This magical moment completes the book I'm publishing
Inner strength, feet planted firmly, no more life stumbling

Chapter Fucking 40
11th Annual Drink Pink 2019 Event

The evening of this event finally arrived. My daughter and her boyfriend, my father and his beautiful girlfriend, my boyfriend, some friends and clients attended in support of me and this wonderful cause. My daughter, my biggest supporter, my biggest fan, ended up wearing a gorgeous gown of mine older than she was and looked absolutely stunning.

Look at how beautiful that was – my daughter was there in the beginning, never left my side and was there to celebrate at the very end of this awful journey. She stuck by my side no matter what. It was a tough journey for both of us. Imagine fearing the loss of your mother, fearing the unknowns, growing up these last four years wondering what will happen if I lose my mother, my best friend in life, the one I'm closest to, the one I can talk to about anything, the one who loves and supports me unconditionally? Cancer affects all those who love you in such horrible ways.

The Lounsbury House, the venue, was lit up in pink for the event. Black and white posters of all of the women, the breast cancer survivors, were on display throughout. Appetizers were being passed around, pink beverages were being served and there was a lot of laughter filling those rooms. Everywhere I looked, there were smiles on peoples' faces. I was surrounded by so much love, especially by my close circle. I found my poster in the center of the room and as I faced it, I realized, I fucking did it! What a momentous time of my life, four plus years later, to see this fierce warrior staring back at me, in print, confirming that this part of my life is fucking over and I fucking survived.

I truly felt like a princess that magical evening. My boyfriend bought me the beautiful pink dress I wore and surprised me that evening with the glamorous bling purse I wanted and a gorgeous bouquet of pink roses. I had my hair and make-up done at Adam Broderick's Salon, my nails blinged out to match the rest of the bling I was wearing, bling earrings, bling necklace, bling diamond bracelet, bling shoes, you name it! Bling and pink goes beautifully together! I felt beautiful, whole and at peace.

Kristen Jensen, my friend and photographer, thought so, too! She looked stunning that evening. Ironically, her dress was bling with a pink shawl. We were color coordinated and never planned it. Kristen has run this event for eleven years now. This year, 2019, the event brought in the most it ever had, over $56,000. All of the money raised goes to Ann's Place, a wonderful local organization that helps those with breast cancer.

Kristen is a kind soul, beautiful inside and out. The amount of time and dedication it took each and every year to be able to put this together is astounding when one thinks about it. Photo shoots for all of the breast cancer survivors, reviewing and editing, designing the posters, the programs, choosing the venue and arranging all the details of the evening are just some of the obvious tasks. The evening was beyond perfect. Tickets on line sold out. Tickets sold like crazy at the door the evening of. The place was packed given the attendance was incredible.

At one point, Kristen and the twelve new courageous face models were introduced by the fabulous comedian Christine O'Leary. We were all standing on the staircase, looking down at the sea of faces and emotion overcame me. I was overwhelmed with the feelings of love, support, the look of love and pride in the eyes of those who love me, the knowledge that I'm not alone and I survived, that this awful journey is over and a new beautiful one was just born. There was so much fucking strength in that room. I felt the tears starting to slip. It was empowering and emotional to stand up there and I have Kristen to thank for that.

Kristen was there to photograph me in the very beginning, just prior to losing my breasts. Kristen then photographed me at the end and invited me to become part of Drink Pink.

Drink Pink was a beautiful ending to a challenging four year journey yet ironically, it marks a new beginning to the rest of my life.

Shit happens in life and although it is often out of our control, we have the power to make the most of our situations. I could have let all of this consume me, destroy me, but I chose not to. I chose to laugh amidst my tears. I chose to forge ahead despite all of my challenges. I chose to smile and embrace every single moment in life, every smell, every hug, every single breath.

I chose to write this book and share my story in the hopes it will help others. I have found myself on a new journey in life. Detours can be an inconvenience but they can bring you to new and wonderful destinations, as I always say.

Welcome to the 11th annual

drink.
pink

AMY FERNANDEZ • CINDY SEVELL • DEB POE • DONNA GARDINER

VENUS SANDERS • TOSHA GORGON • SAM EAGLE • NANCY SHAIL

• ELENA PELEPAKO • JENIPHER LAGANA • KATE SMYTH • KRISTEN HATCHER •

Drink Pink 2019 Pictures

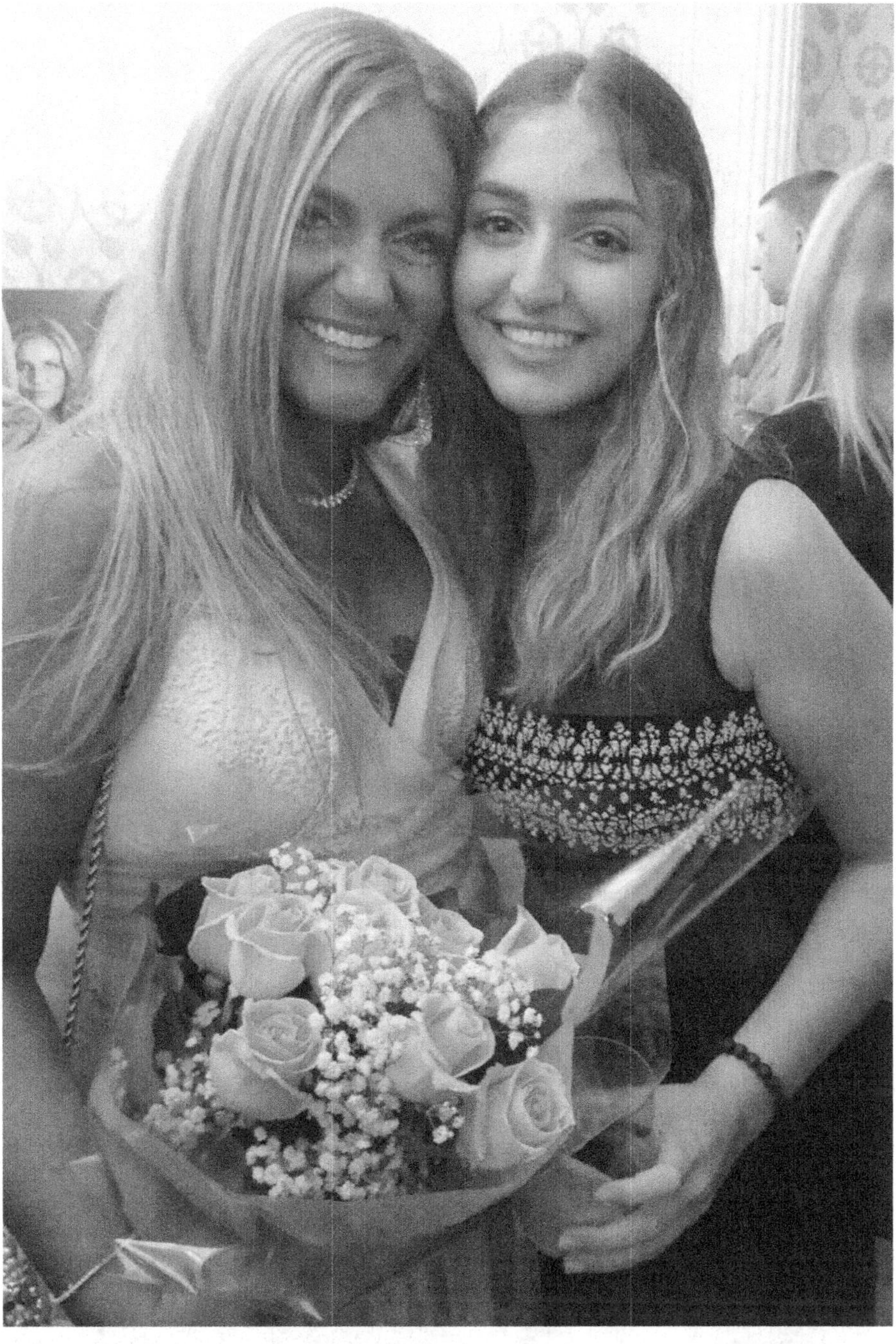

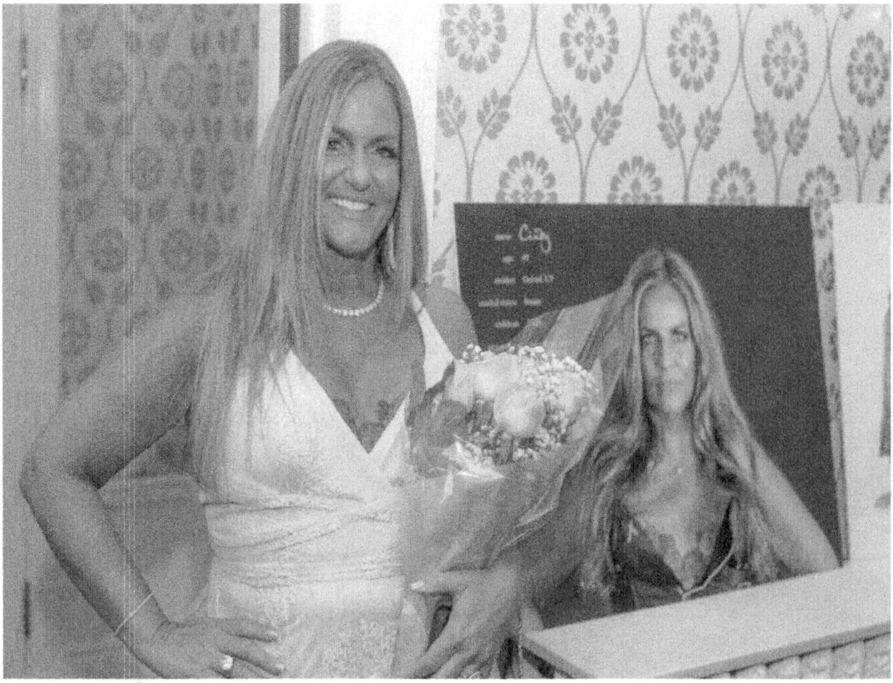

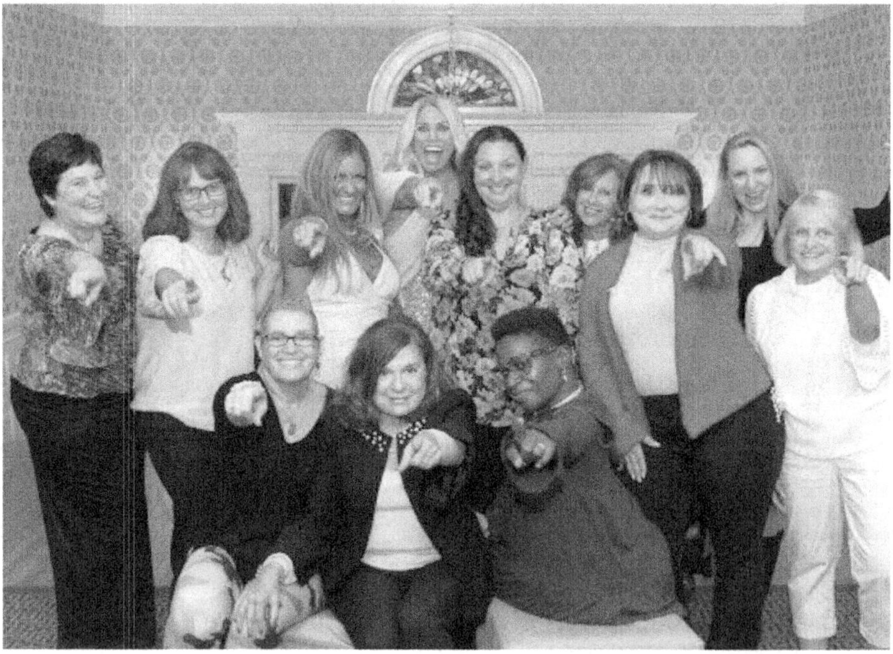

Drink Pink 2019 – Truly A Magical Night

Drink Pink 2019

I fucking did it. I beat cancer.

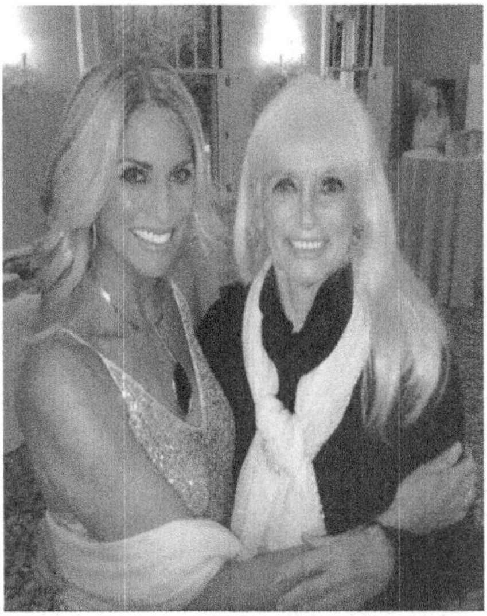
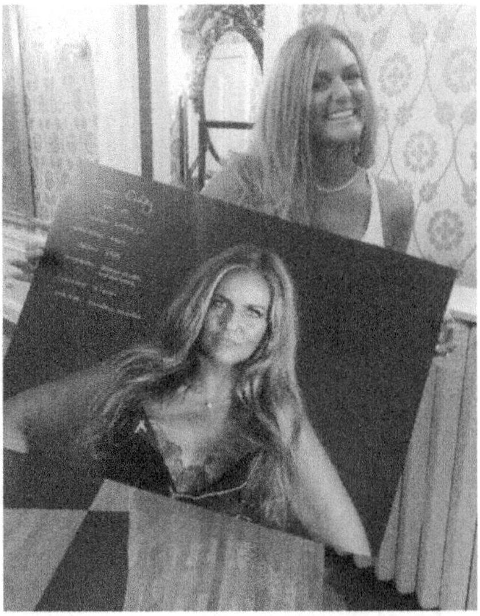
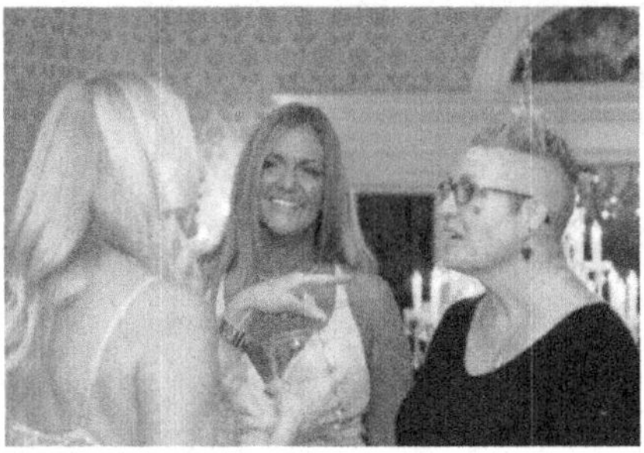
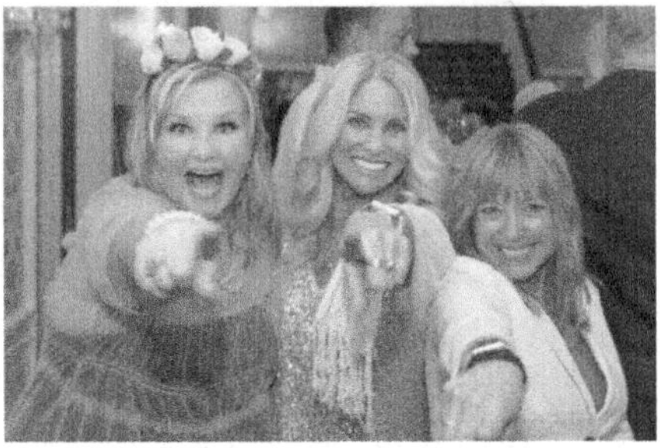
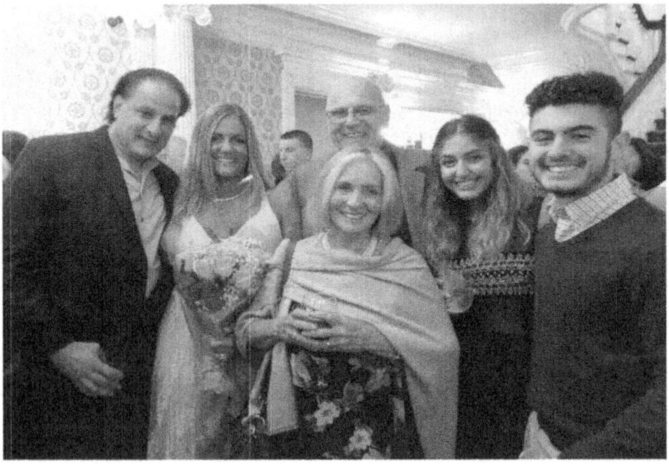

Chapter Fucking 41
Last Fucking Chapter

Done. This book is fucking finished and I have to say, I fucking loved writing it.

Cancer fucking sucks.

FUCKING sucks.

FUCKING SUCKS.

I can't say it any other way. The word cancer is the worst word in the English dictionary. I can think of other "C" words I prefer, such as "cunt", "cockface" or "coochymama". (If you're still reading, I know you can handle these words!)

I know for a fact that all of you, even the most conservative ones who may refuse to read my book given I say it like it is in no diplomatic ways, feel the same way I do about cancer. Cancer just fucking sucks.

I have seen so many books on how to deal with cancer but I honestly couldn't relate to any of them so I decided to write my own in my own fucking way. I know there are others that will relate to my candid thoughts as well as my fucked up journey.

I know how I felt and still do feel about cancer. I fucking hate it. It's one of the worst things anyone can ever hear. What do you do when you're told you or a loved one has cancer? Do you fucking smile? No! That one word changes your life or the life of your loved ones in so many ways. That one word instantly dredges up feelings of fear, sadness and desperation. That one fucking word ends your life as you once knew it and takes you on a whole new journey. That journey isn't fucking easy and can totally rock your world in a pretty shitty way.

Just imagine, you're on a rickety old wooden rollercoaster that knocks you around for a while, flips you upside down, introduces tons of unknown twists and turns, creates havoc on your life for a while, makes you sick and weak, scared, has you begging for it to end, has you holding on for dear life and makes you feel all alone.
I hate those types of rollercoasters in life. But, like any fucking carnival ride, it will eventually STOP.

You'll be able to breathe again. You'll find your footing. You'll feel healthy once again. You'll be able to stand on your own two feet and feel confident and strong. You survived that rollercoaster so you know you can take on any fucking thing that comes your way. You are fucking invincible, my friend! You are ready to take on the world.

You'll get through anything in life because you truly have no choice. The clock will keep ticking so your only choice is to keep moving the fuck forward. No choice here. Your only choice is survival. Do whatever it takes to survive.

I survived and I fucking love my life as it is now. I'm happy. I have two beautiful children in my life. I have a shitload of lessons that inspired me to become the person I am today. I truly feel like a warrior. If I can beat that awful "C" word, I can beat anything. I can accomplish anything. SO CAN YOU.

You don't need to understand everything. You just need to believe in yourself. You need to make yourself your priority. You need to remember to smile no matter the fuck what. You need to find joy in your life. You need to remember the positive no matter how negative your life may seem. You need to keep forging the fuck ahead. A positive mindset, no matter the fuckeries in your life, will help you make your way through. There's a fucking pot of something good waiting for you at the end of your journey.

Life gets better, I fucking promise!!! I hope this book helps give you strength in the face of hardship and brings a fucking smile to your face. Even better if it makes you laugh out loud.

I fucking love to laugh and often amuse myself but in this case, I hope that in sharing my fucked up breast cancer related realities with you, it will help you navigate your own personal journey a little better.

I hope that after reading this book, you will become a stronger, wiser and more positive you.

I hope you use the word "fuck" more often.

In fact, I hope you benefit from my own personal saying.....

IT IS WHAT IT FUCKING IS!!!!!

A few songs and poems written by yours fucking truly...

The Call

Life's short, live fully, embrace every smile
Every scent, every moment, make it worthwhile
Take the good with the bad, create memories today
Grab those you love before time slips away...

The call came in at a quarter to five
Anticipation and dread as I picked up the line
I closed my eyes and let out a big cry
It's not my time to say goodbye...

I gathered my thoughts over the next two weeks
My future was looking pretty bleak
Surgeries, no work, a single Mom
No time to waste let's get this done...

Life's short, live fully, embrace every smile
Every scent, every moment, make it worthwhile
Take the good with the bad, create memories today
Grab those you love before time slips away...

I held my kids close, showered them with love
Prayed to the big man high up above
They need me, I need them, please show me some grace
Lord help me keep this smile on my face...

The surgeries began, not one but eight
Spanning close to four years, was this my fate?
Nightmares and tears consumed our lives
Fears and struggles, I had to survive...

Life's short, live fully, embrace every smile
Every scent, every moment, make it worthwhile
Take the good with the bad, create memories today
Grab those you love before time slips away...

The sun will rise, the sun will set, the questions fall in between
With my head held high
I gaze up to the sky
No one fucks with this queen...

The currents of fear knocked me around but I never lost my drive
Two kids, a life, forced to fight, I had to stay alive
I fought and I fought, I survived and I won
This crazy game with cancer is done!!!

Life's short, live fully, embrace every smile
Every scent, every moment, make it worthwhile
Take the good with the bad, create memories today
Grab those you love before time slips away...

It slips away.....

Pain

It hurts, I ache, I can't catch my breath
My pain is alive, claws gripping my neck
I'm choking, I'm shaking, I can't take anymore
I'm broken, I'm caving, I drop to the floor

I'm gasping for air, reaching for help
I'm curled in a ball, as I let out a yelp
Tears slip down my cheeks, yelps turn to moans
This pain is consuming, I feel so alone

Deep under the grips of the beast
He bares his teeth, he's ready to feast
My body hurts, my heart and my head
I'm gonna explode, they'll find me for dead

Can't get any lower, can't lift myself up
This shitstorm inside is ready to erupt
I need to free myself of this invisible rope
I need a hand, I need some hope

My heart relaxes, my tears slow down
I open my eyes as I look around
I'm at rock bottom, I take a deep breath
I sit myself up, I'm scared to death

Each moment, each day, life keeps going
I'm a hot mess, I'm barely coping
I pull myself up, I stand on my feet
That pain hurts but I'll never know defeat

Cancer, death, illness, divorce
Pain comes at you in full force
One day can flip your world upside down
Just pull up your pants and adjust your crown

Pain attacks our very core
It's a dirty filthy gut wrenching whore
It hurts, it aches, it screams and it drains
Time to break free from its barbed wire chains

Life

Life has a way of beating you down
With boxing gloves, it throws you around
Beats you til you're a hot bloody mess
But don't give up, there's no time for rest

You're down, you're so low, you're in a bad place
You're ready to give up, you're flat on your face
But something is stirring deep within
It's that will to live, you're gonna win

You have the power, to change your life
End all this sorrow, end all this strife
Breathe that air deep, there's life in your lungs
Your heart beats, you have stories unsung

Pick yourself up, dust yourself down
One thing at a time, just look at the now
Little by little, you'll get shit done
One step at a time, your life has begun

Life's full of challenges, it's up to you
It's your choice, what will you do
Curl up and die or stand firm and strong
Choose to stand tall, in the place you belong

Try to smile, see how that feels
It calms the body, it slows time's wheels
Savour today, its smells and its sounds
Each moment alive, each breath above ground

Open your eyes, look all around
The beautiful colors, the blues, pinks and browns
Sunrises awaken the world each day
Hopeful tomorrows bring promises your way

Life's full of happiness, love and laughter
Open your book, it's in your next chapter
Keep turning the pages, it's all perspective
Look for the good, honor and respect it

Life is a journey, with twists and turns
Buckle up tight, just follow those curves
Pedal to the metal, take life full in the face
Success is inevitable when you cut to the chase

A smile on your lips brings light to your eyes
Lifts your attitude, reaches deep inside
Find the good in things, it's there when you look
Keep turning the pages, script your own book

Made in the USA
Monee, IL
13 February 2020